THE PORT OF HONG KONG

A SURVEY OF ITS DEVELOPMENT

T. N. CHIU

HONG KONG UNIVERSITY PRESS

ISBN 0 85656 099 5

Library of Congress Catalog Card Number 73-88376

Printed in Hong Kong by
LIBRA PRESS LIMITED
56 Wong Chuk Hang Road 5D, Aberdeen

THE PORT OF HONG KONG

香港

的

港

口

CONTENTS

PLATES

(*Between pages 70 and 71*)

1   Hong Kong (1842) looking west from above Causeway Bay
2   Victoria Harbour, 1860
3   Victoria waterfront, about 1870
4   Overside delivery of cargo
5   The Western Praya
6   The Ocean Terminal
7   Cross-harbour ferry services
8   The Hong Kong and Kowloon Wharf and Godown Company's
    container complex at Tsim Sha Tsui
9   Reclamation for the container terminal at Kwai Chung

FIGURES

1960 – 1980

TABLES

INTRODUCTION

THE development of a port is not a function of local circumstances alone. Economic and social progress in the area it serves, the rise and fall of rivals and the development of world shipping are all important factors to which a port readily responds.

This is specially true of Hong Kong where, until very recently, there has been little local attraction for trade besides stability and security. It is almost completely devoid of natural resources other than the sheltered, deep-water harbour. All the major advances or setbacks in the evolution of the port have been the results of changes in its external relationships.

From the very beginning, the port inherited the foreign trade of South China with Europe that had been carried on for nearly two centuries. To understand the origin of the port, it is necessary to go beyond the date of its foundation to discover how far it owes its existence to geographical factors and how far to historic accident. Ever since it was founded, the port has been subject to repercussions from events within China proper. Scarcely a decade has passed without new developments, the consequence of rebellion, civil war, invasion, blockade, depression, famine or flood.

In this attempt to explain the development of the port, emphasis is laid only on those events in the port's history that throw the strongest light upon the present scene. For clarity of discussion, the span of the port's development is best divided into five periods:

(1) 1841–98 the establishment of confidence and the foundations of entrepôt trade;
(2) 1899–1940 the development of the China trade up to the outbreak of the Pacific War;
(3) 1941–6 the destruction and rehabilitation of the port;
(4) 1946–50 reconstruction and industrialization;
(5) 1951–70 modernization.

These periods correspond with major changes in external influences on the port. There is no real break in the evolutionary process except for the Pacific War period when the normal function of the port was brought to a sudden halt. The revival of the port at the close of the War was hardly less sudden. Since the War, however, economic and political influences have changed more rapidly, and, in consequence, periods characterized by any one direction of growth have been of shorter duration.

CHAPTER ONE

THE PHYSICAL SETTING

In assessing the influence of the physical setting on the development of the port of Hong Kong, it is important to bear in mind the fact that the port is a recent creation which has not been developed primarily by indigenous people to meet local demands. Hong Kong, before it became a British colony, was not the point where transport by water and by land met. For the accommodation of sailing-ships, the harbour was no more advantageous than the riverine ports of Canton, Whampoa and Macao. Situated in the upper reaches of the Pearl River estuary, Canton and Whampoa were some ninety miles inland from Hong Kong, and at the confluence of three waterways: the Si Kiang, the Pei Kiang and the Tung Kiang (the West, North and East Rivers). With easy access to their hinterland developed through centuries of internal trade, these riverine ports were opened by the Chinese for overseas trade long before Hong Kong's emergence as a port.

The land surrounding Hong Kong harbour was neither productive nor supported a substantial population, while the many inlets and channels among islands and peninsulas became haunts for pirates.[1] The land approach to the port was barred by ranges of hills which were formidable to the primitive means of land transport. However, with the establishment of foreign rule and the application of new techniques and methods of communication, the deep-water shelter of Hong Kong harbour acquired new significance, and Hong Kong eventually intercepted the trade of the Chinese ports. From the point of view of its founders, Hong Kong stood at the junction of routes followed by two different types of maritime carrier: those confined to the China Seas on the one hand, and those that were inter-ocean on the other. Being the only deep-water harbour between Singapore and Shanghai, its capacity to supersede Canton and Whampoa as a transhipment port became evident as the size of ships and the volume of overseas trade grew (Fig. 1).

Hong Kong is geologically and structurally part of the Southeastern Uplands of China which embrace southern Chekiang, the whole of Fukien and much of eastern Kwangtung.[2] This upland region is a remnant of the southern part of the old Cathaysian continent, and

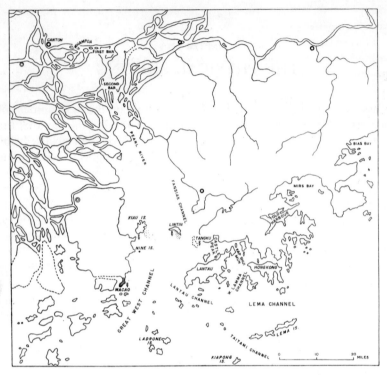

Figure 1. Anchorages for foreign ships in the Pearl River estuary
before 1841.

possesses a well-marked structural pattern of north-east trending ranges
running parallel to the broken coast. Situated at the southern limit of
this ancient massif, Hong Kong exhibits this trend in the long, narrow
inlet at Tolo Harbour and in a main anticlinal fold, both of which run
in a south-west to north-east direction, from Lantau Island across the
centre of the New Territories. This trend finds no expression in the
Hong Kong harbour (Victoria) area but its associated ranges cut across
the landward link of the port with its hinterland. With the exception of
the group of low hills in the Kowloon peninsula, slopes rise steeply from
the coast to over 1,500 feet. The orientation of inland routes from the
port is controlled by high passes. Apart from these the only connection
is by tunnel through more than a mile of solid rock or by circuitous
coastal roads. The difficulty of approach to the port by land is one of the
reasons for the widespread use of junks and river steamers in the

entrepôt trade with the hinterland, a factor which naturally places even more stringent demands on the water site.

The harbour is the centre of a granite cupola which was emplaced with an east-west trend into acid volcanic rocks. Differential erosion on the volcanic and granitic rocks, and on varying structures, grain sizes and textures in the granite, produced the characteristic scarp-like concave slope facing the harbour and the foothills of the Kowloon peninsula and Kwun Tong.[3] Rocky outcrops have been found arranged in a ring around the granite cupola at the foot of the scarp slopes and, in many cases, these establish the limit to urban sprawl. Further away from the hill slopes, and in the centre of the harbour, the land consists of completely weathered granite *in situ*. 'Generally the area below 120 m. (400 ft.) on the north of the harbour is deeply weathered . . . to well over 100 ft. on the low hills. . . . On Hong Kong Island similar conditions exist, the steep hill slopes providing craggy outcrops of rock while low hills are deeply weathered.'[4] The ready availability of fill from the excavation of these weathered materials has facilitated the reclamation of land from the harbour.

The major and final episode in the evolution of Hong Kong harbour was the result of eustatic changes which occurred in the Pleistocene period. Several changes of sea level have left their marks in the form of raised beaches, raised wave-cut platforms and accordant hilltops. From the basin structure of the harbour area it can be seen that the degree of submergence determined the proportion between land space and water space. Confined within an almost complete ring of ridges, which offer both a shelter and a barrier, the one can expand only at the expense of the other. Archaeological finds on raised beaches in and around the harbour area[5] indicate that as recently as late Neolithic times the sea level was from ten to thirteen feet above the present level. A change of this magnitude was sufficient to expose large areas once under shallow water at Tai Kok Tsui, Kowloon Bay and Happy Valley. These areas were the sites of extensive reclamation early in the history of the port's development. This movement also meant that a large part of the harbour was rendered inaccessible to shipping, and reduced the usefulness of the western approach to the harbour.

Hong Kong's seventeen square miles of land sheltered water have been praised as providing one of the world's finest harbours.[6] Hemmed in between the mountainous island of Hong Kong and the Kowloon ranges of hills (Fig. 2), the harbour extends for eight miles in an approximately east-west direction, with widths varying between one and three miles.

Figure 2. Relief map of the Hong Kong harbour area.

The narrowest part lies in the centre, where the Kowloon peninsula stretches southwards in a series of low hills to within one and a quarter miles of the Island, dividing the harbour into two roughly equal halves. By breaking across the eight-mile stretch of water, the peninsula provides further shelter for the western half of the harbour. As the prevailing winds in Hong Kong are easterly, it is evident why the western side of the Kowloon peninsula is the site of the port proper, despite the fact that the eastern half has the deeper water (Fig. 2). The Kowloon peninsula also adds considerably to the length of the protected coastline, giving more space for the development of quays and landing-places. The submergence that formed the harbour gave rise to many branching inlets and bays in the immediate vicinity, notable among which are Aberdeen, Tolo Harbour and Junk Bay. These have functioned separately as shelters for the fleet of harbour-service craft and fishing junks, for laid-up vessels, and for ships too large to enter the harbour. The harbour of Hong Kong, as defined by the water space between the eastern and the western harbour limits (Fig. 19), is thus not the only area in which Hong Kong, as a port, functions: a considerable amount of traffic is handled in smaller outer harbours such as Aberdeen, Stanley, Cheung Chau, Tai O, Deep Bay, Sham Tseng, Tsuen Wan and Sai Kung. These are, however, of local importance only.

There are two entrances to the harbour: Lei Yue Mun to the east and Sulphur Channel to the west. The Lei Yue Mun entrance is over 130 feet deep, but only a quarter of a mile wide; it is used by most ocean-going vessels entering or clearing the harbour. Sulphur Channel is equally narrow but, although it has a depth of more than seventy feet, until recently it was used only by vessels drawing less than twenty-four feet, because of the presence in its approaches of a bar, with a minimum depth of four fathoms. North of Sulphur Channel, the wide opening to the western half of Hong Kong harbour is commonly used by lighter craft. The advantage of this open-passage type of harbour, over the cul-de-sac that is common in harbours formed by coastal submergence, lies in its freedom from silting and from unusually high tidal waves or swells in times of exceptional weather conditions.

With the exception of some shallows at the re-entrants on the coast-line, such as in Kowloon Bay, Hung Hom Bay and between Stonecutters Island and the mainland, the depth of water in the harbour is generally over thirty feet (Fig. 2). The eastern half of the harbour and the main channel running through the centre afford forty feet of draught. Dredging is not required in the harbour except in the immediate vicinity of the south-west tip of the Kowloon peninsula where the largest passenger liners to visit the port are berthed. A large area of the harbour has been dredged, however, with the main object of taking out the sand, which is in great demand for building purposes. The location of these dredging works depends on the presence of the right sort of material under the floor of the harbour and does not necessarily coincide with the shoals.

The areas of shallow water immediately off the coast offer an advantage rather than an impediment to the development of the port. This is largely due to the fact that the spacious water site is not matched by an adequate land site and, in the years since port development started, more than three square miles of shallow water in the harbour have been reclaimed, to provide valuable land. Moreover, anchorages and shelters for small craft, of which the harbour contains a large number, are to be found in these shallow waters.

The approaches to the harbour are by deep channels which, although studded with groups of hilly islands, provide ample room for vessels to reach the harbour without a pilot. Vessels normally direct their course to the Lema Channel, to the south of Hong Kong Island, whence they approach the harbour by an easterly or a westerly route, depending on their size and their berth in the harbour. For ships coming in from the south-west, the Lema Channel is reached by passing between the islands of Ladrone and Kaipong, while for those coming in from the south, it is reached by the Taitami Channel between Kaipong and Lema Islands. The westerly route to the harbour is by the West Lamma Channel, which is over three and a half miles wide. The easterly route is by the Tathong Channel which has a minimum depth of six and a half fathoms, but unlike the western route it is confined by a number of islands and headlands. Rocky reefs, the most prominent among which are the Tathong Rock and Ngai Ying Pai, further restrict the width of the channel, which may be considered absolutely safe for all classes of vessels to a width of half a mile. Owing to greater exposure to easterly winds and its narrower channel, the eastern route is equipped with a series of navigational aids including lighthouses, light-buoys, radar beacons and fog signals. The rocky promontories facing the approach channels are also coated with white cement wash to give easily distinguishable landmarks to vessels.

In order to appreciate the advantage which the deep water in the approach channels and roadsteads offers shipping, the changes in the water-level caused by tides need to be considered. Hong Kong harbour has 'a tidal regime of both mixed semi-diurnal tides and diurnal tides:'[7] that is, for some days of the year, the two daily high tides and the two low tides are all of different heights, yet on a number of days in the year, only one high tide and one low tide are observable. This has been explained as the phenomenon in which the lower high tide merges with, or cancels out, the higher low tide. The range of the tides is less than eight and a half feet, and for most days of the year a range of only five feet is experienced in the harbour. This tidal range has little effect on the navigability of the waters in and around the harbour, which can be entered or cleared at any hour of the day. There are few problems in berthing ships at quays and piers or at moorings in the centre of the harbour. The provision of landing-places for lighters and other harbour craft has been made relatively easy; in most cases it amounts to little more than building a seawall when the land is reclaimed. Abnormal tides are extremely rare in the harbour although they have caused the greatest hazard to shipping and to the port.[8]

Deviation from the normal range is from one foot below the predicted tide level to several feet above it. The effects of exceptionally low tides are felt only by the few users of the harbour for whom a critical minimum draught exists. These tides have been known for example, to delay the launching of ships. On the other hand, exceptionally high tides have caused flooding along the waterfront and, because these are generally accompanied by typhoons, they have caused loss of life and great damage to property. Storm surges or tidal waves, which consist of a rise of water coincident with the approach of a typhoon, are brought about by reduced atmospheric pressure combined with the piling-up of water by the wind. They rarely exceed five feet in open seas, but in confined waters shoaling may add considerably to their height. If the surges coincide with the highest normal high tides in the harbour, the result is devastating. 'The maximum surge height (recorded minus predicted tide) in Hong Kong harbour was about six and a half feet, which could have raised the water-level to fifteen feet above the Chart Datum if it had coincided with a maximum possible predicted tide of eight and a half feet.'[9] Tidal surges do not, however, usually reach such heights. Out of the thirteen storms between 1906 and 1957 for which tidal data are available, seven produced maximum surges of less than four feet, and only two of more than six feet. The configuration of the harbour and its coastal contours have contributed much to reduce the dangers of such surges. The constricted entrance on the east, from which direction most of the high winds and heavy seas reach the harbour, the divergence of the coastline immediately inside the entrance, and the wide-open western approaches to the harbour are therefore all important features of the water site.

As Hong Kong harbour lies at the mouth of the Pearl River and as it is open at both the eastern and the western ends, it forms one of the channels through which tidal streams of the Pearl River pass. Observations on tidal movements made by Hulse[10] provide a picture of tidal streams which is reproduced in Figure 3. A large proportion of the ships using the port berth at moorings in the middle of the harbour. The effect of the daily reversal of flow directions is such that these ships tend to swing at their moorings in the direction of the tidal flow, but not at the same rate. Moorings have thus to be so spaced that two ships berthed at adjoining buoys can never strike each other. It is evident that this practice of anchoring midstream is most space-consuming and one that would be impracticable in a less spacious water site.

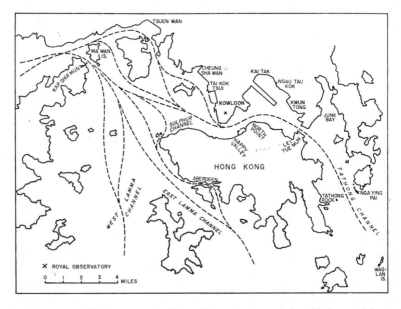

Figure 3. Tidal streams in Hong Kong harbour (after Hulse, 1960).

Tidal currents are strongest at the two constrictions, namely Lei Yue Mun and Kap Shui Mun, where the average flow runs at two to three knots and four to five knots respectively. Other spots in the harbour where a strong current flows are through the narrow gap between the Kowloon peninsula and Hong Kong Island, off North Point, and south of Stone-cutters Island. Hulse observed that the ebb flow could be very strong after heavy rain had fallen in the Pearl River delta, when there occurred an east-south-easterly spate from Kap Shui Mun running south of Stonecutters Island into the harbour. The merging of the higher low tide and the lower high tide produces no definite flow direction in the water although a very slow circulating movement in the western harbour is observable. When the tide streams flow there are some minor reverse currents or eddies near the shore at Kennedy Town, off Wan Chai, Hung Hom, Aldrich Bay and west of the Kowloon peninsula.

One of the combined effects of the strength and direction of the tidal streams is to preserve the depth of the harbour. An important contribution to this effect is the absence of large streams entering the harbour area which might bring down considerable quantities of debris. Silting is not a problem in the conservancy of the port. The need to maintain the natural scour by tidal streams, however, is being carefully watched; it was one of the reasons for building the tidal model of Hong Kong harbour at the Hydraulics Research Station at Wallingford, Berkshire, where changes in the tidal stream caused by large-scale harbour works were investigated. An increase in the scour of the streams is also undesirable because the floor of the harbour provides one of the main sources of sand in Hong Kong. Erosion of the harbour floor might weaken the hold of the mooring-buoys, while sedimentation might reduce the depth of the anchorage. It is the business of the port conservators to ensure that the equilibrium is maintained between scour and deposition.

The association of extraordinarily high water-levels with typhoons has been mentioned. In this connection it is worth noting that Hong Kong lies on one of the paths frequented by typhoons in the China Seas (Fig. 4). Typhoons are in fact the greatest physical disadvantage in the port's location both because of their unpredictability and because of the large-scale damage they cause. Owing to the erratic nature of the move-ment, force and frequency of typhoons that may affect the harbour, there are as yet no means of safeguarding shipping in the port apart from a warning system, breakwaters for light craft and heavier chains for mooring-buoys. These precautionary measures have been found useful during the passage of most typhoons and during periods of strong monsoon, but they are quite inadequate against a direct hit. Since very little is known about the upper atmospheric circulation over the China

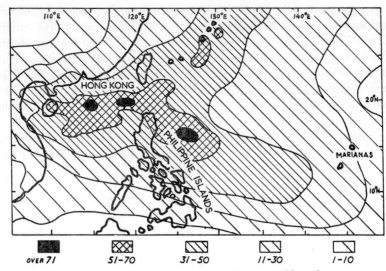

Figure 4. Frequency of occurrence of typhoons, 1884–96, 1905–39, 1946–47 (after Starbruck, Hong Kong Royal Observatory, 1951).

Seas—which is believed to be the force governing the movement of typhoons—forecasts are based mainly on experience.[11]

Although typhoons have been known to occur in the Far East in every month of the year, none has affected Hong Kong in the period between December and May of any year. While most typhoons recorded in Hong Kong have occurred in September, there is no relation between the severity of a typhoon and the month of the year in which it occurs: the typhoon of 9 June 1960, for example, was not only one of the earliest of that year but also one of the most devastating on record.[12] There have been many years in which no typhoons have been recorded while in others there have been as many as four. Correlations have been found[13] to exist between high wind speed and high sea levels. The greatest surge occurs when the centre of a westward-moving typhoon passes over Hong Kong or within seven nautical miles to the south. The surge usually occurs within one hour before the wind maximum and three hours after it. Mean wind speeds of forty-five knots or less do not produce surges greater than two and a half feet, but the surge tends to be unusually high when it is accompanied by heavy rain and when the passing typhoon is fast-moving. These observations show that all the meteorological elements in a typhoon combine to create its power of destruction. Although it is impossible to determine how much of the damage can be ascribed to tides and how much to winds, by far the heaviest damage is done on, or near, the water.

Since there is a correlation between the direction from which typhoons approach and surge heights, it is worth noting that all but three of the sixty-two typhoons recorded in a period of fifty-three years have approached from the south-east quadrant. Those that have passed to the north or north-east had already been moving across the mainland at the time of their nearest approach. Much of their energy had been spent and they were less serious threats to the harbour than those that have followed a sea track. However, it is not often that the tracks of typhoons have passed within seven nautical miles to the south, and their centres have usually not been fast-moving.

Another meteorological phenomenon that significantly detracts from the usefulness of the natural harbour (and the airport it contains, one of the largest in the Far East) is fog. Fogs along the South China coast are of the sea-fog type which occur most frequently in late winter and early spring, but rarely at other times of the year (Table 1). They are observed during breaks in the northerly monsoon when tropical air

TABLE 1. TOTAL NUMBER OF FOG DAYS AT WAGLAN ISLAND, THE ROYAL OBSERVATORY AND AT KAI TAK AIRPORT, 1948–50

Station	Jan	Feb	Mar	Apr	May	Jun	Jul	Aug	Sept	Oct	Nov	Dec	Total
Waglan	12	20	16	12	4	—	—	—	—	—	—	4	68
Royal Observatory	11	13	9	8	1	—	—	—	—	—	—	1	43
Kai Tak	3	11	7	4	1	—	—	—	—	—	—	1	27

SOURCE: Hong Kong Royal Observatory, *Fogs at Waglan Island and their Relationship to Fogs in Hong Kong Harbour,* by K. R. Hung, 1951.

which has travelled over warm seas to the east or south reaches the cooler waters along the coast.[14] The greatest contrasts between air temperature and sea temperature, and hence the greatest probability of fog formation, are associated with southerly winds. Most fogs observed in the harbour of Hong Kong are formed in the open seas and drift into the harbour through the eastern entrance. This movement of fog has been reported by Hung,[15] based on observations of fog in the harbour and on Waglan Island—a small island nine miles to the south-east of the harbour. It has been found that the ranges of hills surrounding the harbour shelter it from the north-east and the south-east, so that fogs have been observed on fewer occasions at the Royal Observatory at the southern end of the Kowloon peninsula than at Waglan Island. Kai Tak airport has had even fewer observations because it lies farther back in the 'shadow' of the hills. 'When a fog drifts in through the Lei Yue Mun Pass from Waglan, it will mostly be blown westwards by the prevailing easterly wind in the harbour, and often crosses the tip of the Kowloon peninsula, reducing visibility at the Royal Observatory. On the other hand, for fog to drift into the head of Kowloon Bay and over Kai Tak, the wind in the harbour must be southeast. However, this direction is critical for the passage of fog through Lei Yue Mun, since the eastern end of Hong Kong Island then exerts a blocking effect, with the result that fog no longer enters the harbour.'[16]

CHAPTER TWO

FOUNDATIONS OF THE ENTREPÔT TRADE

THE Colony of Hong Kong did not have a large population to start with: in 1841 it was a barren island with a few mat-sheds for fishermen. Underlying its subsequent development as a port is a long history of international trade, and from this trade came the justification for its initial growth. At the time of Hong Kong's cession to the British Government in 1841, it had been repeatedly stated that the aim of the occupation was for diplomatic, military and commercial purposes.[1] Diplomatic and military purposes were, however, only the means to an end, which was commerce. It should be pointed out that foreign trade at Canton, the only port where Europeans were allowed to trade in the late eighteenth century, was not started for the development of the hinterland, but for the revenue and profit it would bring the merchants and the local authorities. Foreign merchants made their profit from the sale of tea and silk in their home countries; their cargoes of cotton and woollen goods were sold at a loss in Canton.[2] Opium was not important until the 1780s, almost two and a half centuries after the first British ship traded in China. The Co-Hong system, the Canton merchant guild founded in 1720, was the device by which exactions could be effectively made from the merchants, both foreign and Chinese. Such commercial relationships could hardly continue with the growth of the spirit of free trade in the early nineteenth century. The British merchants, having secured the abolition of the monopoly when the charter of the East India Company expired on 22 April 1834, were thereafter bent on lowering the trade barrier on the Chinese side.

Starting from small beginnings in 1715, when trade with Canton was put on a regular footing, the East India Company grew and developed throughout the eighteenth century. Until the first quarter of the nineteenth century, it completely dominated China's commercial relationships with Western powers. The influence of the Portuguese at Macao was on the decline. Although the Portuguese were the first European traders to become established on Chinese soil, their sovereignty at Macao was not recognized until 1887, and this to a great extent accounted for their lack of vigour in developing its port facilities. By the beginning of the nineteenth century, Macao had already ceased to be an important trading station. Its importance was as a smuggling centre for opium and as a rendezvous for Chinese emigrants, both the opium trade and emigration being prohibited by the Chinese Government. During this time, Chinese trade with Japan, Formosa, Indo-China, Siam, the Philippines and other islands in the East Indies continued to expand, and was carried on in large Chinese junks. This coastal junk traffic reached from Tientsin in the north to Hainan in the south. From Canton, cargoes went to Goa in Portuguese ships, to Pondicherry in French, to Bombay and Calcutta in British and Dutch, and to London, Quebec, Halifax, the Persian Gulf, St Helena and New South Wales in British and American ships. Swedish and Danish ships also competed in this carrying trade. All except the British and Americans had ceased to be important carriers by 1820. Detailed information on trade is scanty for this period. The accounts of the East India Company provide a good picture not only of the British share in the China trade but also of the American. The Company's records do not, however, represent the whole of British trade, for a considerable amount of private trading was carried out by personnel on the ships; this may have amounted to as much as one-third of the Company's venture.

Cargoes imported at Canton may be grouped into two categories: those brought directly from Europe, and those brought from India and the East Indies. In the first group were woollen goods, broadcloth, longells and camlets, together with some lead, copper and tin. In the second group were raw cotton and piecegoods, opium from Bombay, pepper and rice from Malaya and the East Indies, and other highly miscellaneous goods such as elephant tusks, birds' nests, rattan and tortoise-shell. China's exports were tea, silk, sugar, China root, tutenag (spelter), vermilion and treasure (silver), and small quantities of articles like camphor, cassia, nankeens, lacquer ware, chinaware, grass-cloth and produce of the Cantonese craftsmen. Among these lists of commodities, only three—tea, silk and opium—had any real significance. In the last few years of its monopoly, the Company's sole export from China was tea. The export of silk was restricted by the Chinese Government and, to meet the high demand, silk was smuggled by way of the Lintin receiving ships. The opium trade, being contraband, was completely outside the Company's accounts. It was the Company's policy to confine itself to the production of opium in India and not to participate in its distribution in China. Consumption of Indian opium rose from 17,760 chests (valued at $12,000,000) in 1830, to 26,000 chests (valued at $17,000,000) in 1835.[3] This shows that the price fell as the amount imported increased. New markets had to be opened outside the Canton area. In 1832, the firm of Jardine Matheson and Company, which was (and still is) one of the leading private merchant houses in the China trade, took the initiative in sending ships to Shanghai, Tientsin, Amoy and Foochow and in laying down a fleet of 'clippers' for the Calcutta-Lintin run. They were soon followed by rival firms.

The only comprehensive account of the trade at Canton is to be obtained from the shipping figures recorded by the East India Company, which covered all foreign ships. These show a continuous increase in the number of ships loading at Canton; in 1833, the final year of the record, there were 189 ships, of which 107 were British. The first few years of free trade after 1833 saw a rapid increase in the imports of opium and British manufactured goods. In addition to the need for new markets, there arose another, pressing need for bigger and more secure storage facilities. When hostilities between China and Great Britain broke out in 1839, there was an immediate demand for a base for naval operations and a garrison for troops. Hong Kong was to meet all these demands.

The trading activities of the East India Company at Canton, Macao, Amoy, Chusan and Ningpo, and the course of events leading to the war of 1839-41, have been detailed in the major works of Morse, Bernard, Eitel and others.[4] A study of their accounts throws light on the factors that caused Britain to seek the possession of territory on the China coast and on the reasons for its ultimate choice of a site.

The first factor was the need for security, a prerequisite for trade. The extortions exacted by the Chinese authorities, the humiliation imposed by stringent regulations, and the inconvenience of having to leave the factory every winter, all led to a desire for a trading-post under the British Government. The idea of having an insular position for such a trading-post was connected with the problem of its defence. An island with a deep and sheltered anchorage was ideal in the nineteenth century, when British naval power was supreme in the Far East. Separation from the Chinese community had been found desirable for sanitary reasons and for the maintenance of law and order.[5] It was not by coincidence that foreign settlements in Canton, Amoy, Foochow and Shanghai had the common topographical feature of lying 'not only on the water but behind a defensive screen of water.'[6]

The second factor was the example set by the enviable position of the Portuguese in Macao. By establishing a trading-post so close to the Chinese authorities, they were able to claim preferential treatment and to intervene when other European traders appeared on the China scene. The inhospitality experienced by the British merchants when they sought refuge in Macao in the winter seasons must have deeply impressed on their minds the advantage of having a station of their own.

Before 1757, when Canton was made the only port where foreign trade was permitted, British merchants had established factories on the islands of Taiwan, Amoy and Chusan. There the Europeans were less under Chinese control and had more opportunity for independent action. Such island positions compared very favourably with Canton, which was accessible only by a long channel of difficult navigation (Fig. 1).[7] The anchorages around Hong Kong were not strange to the foreign sailing-ships, having provided refuge for them year after year: the season for ships to arrive was in the months August to October, when the typhoon season was not yet over. As evidenced by the records of the East India Company, Hong Kong harbour was visited as early as 1689 by the *Defence,* and the *Carolina* did clandestine trade at the island of Lantau. It was also the place of rendezvous for Lord Amherst's Embassy to China in 1816–17, and for the Company's ships after 1816. The first suggestion that Hong Kong be taken as a trading residence, like Macao for the Portuguese, was made in 1781 by James Bradshaw, the Company's chief supercargo. As the restrictions on trade became less bearable, the clamour for taking possession of 'a detached island' grew.[8] In 1829–30, the Committee of the Company at Canton put an embargo on trade, sending away its ships in protest against restrictions and injustice. One result of this 'revolt' was an examination of several anchorages in which ships might be sheltered. At the outset all were ordered to Tangku Roads (Fig. I). Finding insufficient shelter from south-west winds in Tangku, it was finally decided to bring the ships into Hong Kong harbour and Kap Shui Mun. Cargoes were discharged and loaded.

It thus seems clear that a fair knowledge of the perils to shipping and areas of refuge off the South China coast existed at the beginning of the nineteenth century. Geographical considerations did play an important part in the choice of the 'detached island'.

The prohibition by Chinese imperial edict of the import of opium in 1800 was the direct cause of the growth of transhipment services around Hong Kong. Ships carrying opium thereafter anchored regularly at Lintin, Nine Island or Kap Shui Mun where they unloaded their cargo of opium into receiving ships which, in fact, were strongly-fortified floating warehouses. The ships then went up the Pearl River to carry on legitimate trade. From the receiving ships the opium was delivered into fast boats (called fast crabs) and transported south as far as Hainan and north as far as Tientsin. The trade thus involved considerable break of bulk and grading (because of adulteration). It could well be argued that an entrepôt trade, with all its regular elements such as warehouses, lighters and stevedoring services, had been generated. The magnitude of this transhipment service may be realized by noting that between 1800 and 1821 the annual import of opium was about 5,000 chests: it rose to 16,500 chests in 1831, and to 40,000 chests in the season 1838–9.[9] Opium was not the only cargo that required transhipment. When the Company's ships anchored in Hong Kong harbour and Tangku Roads, all their cargoes, including cotton and woollen manufactures, were transhipped and went up to Canton under other flags. The American firm of Russell and Company organized a regular service between Hong Kong and Whampoa, and British ships at Hong Kong were able to obtain cargoes of tea for their homeward journey. There was a great demand for such a service. 'Freight for this short route rose to $6 per bale of cotton to be carried to Whampoa and $10 per ton for Chinese produce from Whampoa to the British ships.'[10]

When the decision had to be made as to which island should be occupied, Hong Kong was the obvious choice in the minds of those who had first-hand knowledge of existing physical and commercial conditions. The following remarks were made by a correspondent of the *Canton Register*: 'If the lion's paw is to be put down on any part of the south side of China, let it be Hong Kong; let the lion declare it to be under his guarantee a free port, and in ten years it will be the most considerable mart east of the Cape. The Portuguese made a mistake: they adopted shallow water and exclusive rule. Hong Kong, deep water, and a free port for ever!'[11] The larger island of Lantau was recommended by many instead of Hong Kong Island. The principal objection to it was its extent, which would make it more difficult to hold against an enemy, especially pirates. Its more exposed anchorage and its lack of an abundant freshwater supply also militated against this choice. Dissatisfaction about the choice of the island of Hong Kong was only expressed by people who had little experience of the actual state of affairs at Canton.[12]

Establishment of the Settlement and its Early Development

The morphology of the Island at the time of cession is well described by Bernard and Eitel, the former illustrating the description by a chart, which shows the relief of the Island with remarkable accuracy. The

Island and its surrounding waters were also surveyed by Captain Belcher of H.M.S. *Sulphur,* in 1841. Part of the map constructed from this survey is reproduced in Figure 5 to show the original coastline, which was to change beyond recognition within twenty years. Early visitors to the Island invariably described Hong Kong as composed of barren rocks, deep ravines and mountain torrents, with native buildings scattered along the foreshore: 'although beautiful in the distance from its form and outline, it is sterile and unpromising upon close examination.'[13] From the shore, hill slopes rose steeply to over 1,000 feet, giving no coastal flats. Along the northern shore of the Island there used to be a narrow bridle-path extending from West Point to East Point; the latter, and Wong Nai Chung (Happy Valley) to its east, were among the first Chinese settlements on the Island. The development of the settlement was very much dictated by the relief, and the east-west extent of the city of Victoria (the name given to the settlement in 1843) was striking from the beginning. The Island was first occupied by naval forces at Possession Point where, on a small mound, the British flag was hoisted on 26 January 1841. It was immediately followed by the building of barracks, batteries and naval stores. The western and eastern extremities of Victoria Bay apparently proved most unhealthy to Europeans, the centre less so.

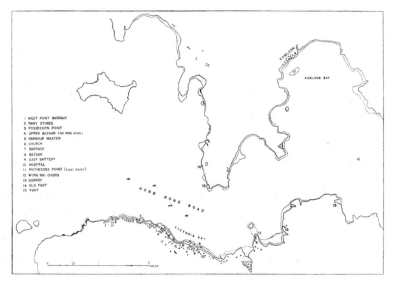

Figure 5. Hong Kong (Queen's Town) in 1841.

At the recommendation of a health committee, the ground in the neighbourhood of West Point was levelled and well drained. To the east, several houses had been built in 1843 upon the lower slopes of Wong Nai Chung, in the expectation that this would be the site of a second town when all available space along the front of Victoria Bay was occupied. However, the unhealthy conditions caused by the swamp in the valley made the area unsuitable for habitation, and the business settlement moved gradually westwards. This seems to explain the early concentration of development in what is today the central district of the city. The most active urban development took place between Possession Point and Murray Battery.

In February 1841, immediately following the occupation of the Island, many parties of British and foreign merchants and missionaries came over from Macao to select sites for warehouses and residences. The barren island provided no timber for construction so that wooden houses had to be imported from Singapore and put on lower storeys of brick or stone. At the eastern end large, stone quarries which had been worked for a long time by skilled Chinese labourers much facilitated building work. Most of the buildings erected during the first two years, however, were merely mat-sheds or wooden houses with stone bases. It was a significant indication of the early attention given to port works for trading that the first substantial buildings put up by private enterprise were the warehouses (godowns) of Lindsay and Company at Wan Chai and of Jardine Matheson and Company at East Point.

Chinese labourers, skilled and unskilled, were required for all sorts of construction work. Most of them came from Kowloon across the harbour. They were followed by a considerable influx of Chinese merchants, provision dealers and artisans, crowding in the bazaar opposite the present naval yard and around the market (Fig. 5). Their settlements grew at Tai Ping Shan, Sai Ying Pun (literally, West Point Barracks) and Tsim Sha Tsui.

Queen's Road, the first road in the Colony, was completed in 1842, joining East Point and West Point and following closely the shape of the foreshore. It was extended to Sai Wan in 1845 and to Aberdeen, on the south side of the Island, in 1846. Along the whole of the distance, at intervals, buildings were going up. The great distance from one end of Victoria to the other was already a source of much inconvenience, and the desirability of a quay along the front of the harbour grew as the settlement became increasingly crowded. Figure 6 shows the irregular waterfront—the result of piecemeal development by marine lot holders.

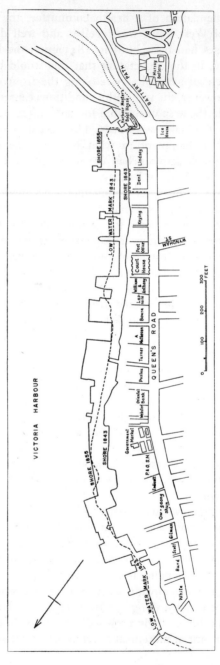

Figure 6. Victoria waterfront between 1843 and 1855 (after Tregear and Berry).

Lack of definite control over the extension of these lots by reclamation and by the construction of seawalls or quays led to much legal dispute in the following years. As it was, in 1843 the back of the warehouses in most instances faced the water, detracting from the appearance of the town as seen from the harbour.[14]

A grave lack of suitable land for urban expansion was felt in the second decade of growth, which saw a sudden immigration of Chinese, fleeing from disorder in the neighbouring provinces. In 1854, the Surveyor-General reported the necessity of extending the city along the shore to the west, as in that locality were to be found the only valuable spots now left for carrying on trade with facility.[15] Again, in 1855, he advocated the expansion of the city to the east, beyond the Albany Godowns at Wan Chai, and the reclamation of land from the sea in front of Bonham Strand. The fill he reckoned to obtain by removing the hill at Possession Point; the level ground so obtained 'might provide for upwards of a hundred houses and with the extension of the land seawards, an additional frontage of 1,800 feet is obtained . . . giving accommodation to at least 3,000 Chinese.'[16] This method of reclamation, by excavating into the hills and filling in the sea, is still being employed to provide land in the Colony. In 1855, however, the opposition of the marine lot holders was so great that the proposal was defeated. Except for the reclamation of the Wong Nai Chung valley, partly by filling in and partly by draining, no major reclamation was carried out until 1868.

Work was started in 1868 on the construction of a 2,700 feet seawall, extending from Wilmer Street to Bonham Strand West and on the reclamation of the sea behind. Piecemeal construction carried out by private interests and by the Public Works Department was done east of Bonham Strand, so that by 1873 a more or less continuous praya ran along the present site of Des Voeux Road. There followed a period of active reclamation and praya construction. The major works were at Causeway Bay, adding twenty-three acres in 1884, and at Kennedy Town, adding twenty-two acres in 1886. The Praya Reclamation Scheme of 1889, the biggest undertaken to that date, provided a strip in the central district, 250 feet wide extending 3,400 yards along the coast, and giving the western end of the city its present shape.

Great changes in the shape of the harbour were also made on the northern shore along the western and eastern fringes of the Kowloon peninsula, after its acquisition in 1860. Guided by the experience of opening up the Island, development in Kowloon showed much more forethought. As on the Island, construction was carried out by private enterprise, but more control was exercised by the Government. Conditions attached to the sale of land made sure that no acute overcrowding was allowed to develop. The gridiron pattern of the roads in the Tsim Sha Tsui and Yau Ma Tei areas of Kowloon contrasts strongly with the sinuous streets of the West Point and Tai Ping Shan districts of the Island. Planning was facilitated by the favourable physiography of the peninsula. Kowloon consisted of rolling ground where low 'compartmented hills'[17] of weathered debris provided convenient fill for reclamation. These hills regulated development. Tsim Sha Tsui, Yau Ma Tei, and Hung Hom were first developed into small settlements separated by hilly ground. Road connections for these three were not provided until the end of the nineteenth century. As these towns expanded, link roads were cut into the hills, providing more material for reclamation. At the end of the period, Yau Ma Tei had extended to the north and merged with Mong Kok and Tai Kok Tsui (Figs. 7 and 8).

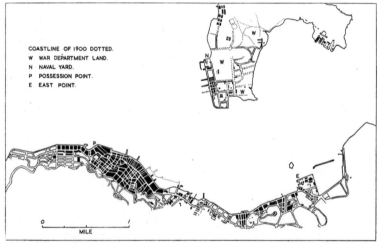

COASTLINE OF 1900 DOTTED.
W WAR DEPARTMENT LAND.
N NAVAL YARD.
P POSSESSION POINT.
E EAST POINT.

MILE

Figure 7. Victoria and Kowloon in 1888.

The most persistent obstacle to the development of the port was the occupation of extensive areas in the centre of the city by military establishments. The Colony was founded during a period of intensive military operations on the China coast, when large naval stores, barracks and batteries were required. At a time when even the permanency of the port was in question,[18] the military use of such land was not considered

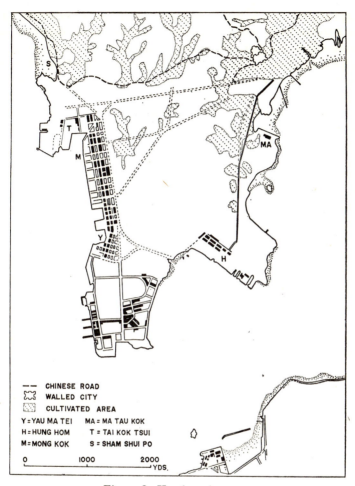

Figure 8. Kowloon in 1900.

in any way detrimental. Since the Chinese Government maintained its antagonistic attitude and continued to threaten the safety of the foreign settlements until well into the twentieth century, British military dominance could not be allowed to lapse. The result was that the military station became so firmly established that, by 1888, the cost of taking down and re-erecting the buildings was too great to allow any proposed removal.[19] The Navy which had been occupying land at West Point as well as in the centre of Victoria Bay, gave up the former in 1854 but only to take up a more convenient position in the centre of the town.[20] Repeated efforts by the colonial Government to bring that part of Victoria City between Government House and Arsenal Street into use for regular civilian purposes and to dislodge the Navy were of no avail.

In Kowloon, guided again by the experience on the Island, the colonial Government tried to restrict military claims as soon as the peninsula was ceded in October 1860. Sir Hercules Robinson, Governor from 1859 to 1865, pointed out that the peninsula was needed to provide storage and docks, as well as to relieve congestion in the city of Victoria. By the decision of the home Government, however, the Army still retained one of the most valuable sites (Fig. 7). Nevertheless, Robinson was able to save land adjoining deep water on the north-west side of Tsim Sha Tsui. This part of the harbour was to become the most important area of the port for deep-water berths and warehouses.

Development of Port Facilities

Warehouses were among the first buildings to appear on the Island, and early descriptions of the port all refer to the extent of warehouse building as evidence of the growth and prospects of trade. On the other hand, there is a lack of records concerning wharf and quay construction. There is sufficient evidence, from the 1845 ordnance map, and from various collections of paintings and sketches of the Colony,[21] to show that, by 1845, Jardine Matheson and Company, by developing the East Point promontory, were able to offer deep-water berths to their own ships. Elsewhere on the Island, facilities for the transport of goods were limited to landing piers and prayas for junks and lighters. There were several reasons for this lack of development. One was that the long-established practice of overside delivery of cargo from ship to lighters had been found satisfactory because of the abundant supply of cheap labour. Time economy meant little in the days of sailing-ships.[22] Again, the policy of the Government was to leave the development of the fore-shore to the merchant houses. There was no co-ordinated effort and, when it was attempted in 1855 (Sir John Bowring's scheme), commercial interests were able to influence its defeat in the Legislative Council. Finally, the indefinite harbour limit made it impossible to estimate the extent to which the waterfront on the Island would be utilized by shipping. Kowloon was still Chinese territory although shipping began to use that side of the harbour from the early days.

The Chinese had their own arrangements for storing goods. Ware-houses were usually on the ground floors or basements of the 'Hong' premises. With the increase in the size of ships and cargoes coming to Hong Kong special buildings had to be built for storage. West Point and Wan Chai were the sites for godowns, as such warehouses were called. As the demand for storage facilities increased, these Chinese godowns began to take in goods for customers and friends. In 1871, the first public godowns came into existence, with the establishment of the Hong Kong Wharf and Godown Company, which made use of landing piers and jetties, and premises at Wan Chai. It was about this time that the old Chinese method of handling cargo was found to be increasingly unsatisfactory. Also, the exactions of the Chinese 'coolie hongs' (porters' guilds) and boat people were becoming intolerable. The newly-formed Company was obliged to build its own lighters, and even to import its own labourers from Swatow and house them on the Company's premises, to free them from the influence of the guilds. In this way, the Company gradually built up a service not only for storage but also for lighterage and cargo delivery within the harbour. In 1875 the foreshore at Tsim Sha Tsui was developed by the Company, and by 1888 two wharves (Nos. 1 and 2) on this site provided deepwater berths for ocean-going ships (Fig. 7).

The development of shipbuilding and ship-repairing facilities was started early and much attention was given to maintaining this service at a high standard. Captain Sand's slip at East Point was able to accommodate ships of up to 300 tons in 1846. As the demand for ship-repairing services rose, so the efforts to meet it increased. The decade after 1857 saw the construction of five dry docks.[23] However, by the 1870s, sailing-ships were fast disappearing from the shipping scene, and steamers with steel hulls were growing in size. The facilities of the Hong Kong docks were unable to accommodate the large mail steamers of the Peninsular and Oriental Company and of the Compagnie de Messageries Maritimes, which had to be sent to Whampoa for docking. In 1880 difficulties arose in placing H.M.S. *Audacious* in the Hope Dock and, as the British Admiralty was contemplating sending larger vessels to the China station, a decision was reached to have a new dock built. This dock, the No. 1 or Admiralty Dock, completed in 1888 at Hung Hom, proved invaluable to the later development of the port. Not only did it provide docking facilities for ships trading to Hong Kong, it also attracted those ships seeking repairs in Far Eastern waters.[24] However, the ship-repairing industry expanded so much before the end of the century that it became necessary to work the establishments of the dock company (then the only one in the Colony) almost day and night, and the building of a larger dock had to be considered.

Apart from the dockyards, the godowns and the wharves, very little had been done to improve shipping activities in the harbour. The Government provided navigation lights, mooring-buoys, meteorological information for shipping and shelter for small craft in typhoon shelters, but it did not play the leading part in port development. It was left to private interests to provide all else that was necessary.[25] To a great extent, this reflected the strong influence of the commercial community over the management of the port. There was confidence in the power of the port to attract trade but also a strong belief that government regulation or control might tend to weaken the attraction.

Economic Development of the Port

The development of the port of Hong Kong is closely associated with the fluctuations of population and trade. Population figures for the early years were at best estimates. They were greatly affected by the dates they were made and especially by the estimates, whether they immediately followed or preceded an influx of Chinese from the mainland. The influence of this movement of people, with their trade, is, however, important.

By an official proclamation signed on 7 June 1841, the Chinese traders were openly invited to trade and stay in Hong Kong, 'where they will receive full protection from the high officers of the British nation; and Hong Kong being on the shores of the Chinese Empire, neither will there be any charges on imports and exports to the British Government.' The Chinese people soon saw the opportunities for trade and employment offered by security and order while the junk trade in the Pearl River was still disrupted by the war of 1841. The Chinese population on the Island was estimated by Eitel at 5,650 in 1841, rising to 19,009 in 1844 and to 22,466 in 1847.

A further step to secure the confidence of the mercantile community was the land sale held early in June 1841. British merchants had begun building without waiting for the confirmation of British sovereignty, many of them having removed their offices from Canton to Hong Kong. The opening of the five treaty ports—Canton, Amoy, Foochow, Ningpo and Shanghai—raised their hopes high. As the first Governor, Pottinger, stated: 'The Treaty of Nanking had opened up a new world to their trade so vast that all the mills of Lancashire could not make stocking stuff for one of its provinces.'[26] The permanency of the Colony was assured when the headquarters of the British Superintendency of Trade were moved there from Macao in 1842. This was accompanied by an influx of British and Portuguese merchant houses from Macao, which added new strength to the business community.

The rapid increase in population, however, was not accompanied by a proportionate growth in trade. In 1850, the home Government received very pessimistic statements of the Hong Kong situation just before the vote was taken for the estimates for the civil establishment and expenses of the Colony. Ships came to Hong Kong from England merely 'to receive instructions from agents, land some house stores for the different shopkeepers, and to discharge a portion of their cargo which may not be immediately required in Canton, ultimately to find its way to Shanghai. Vessels from India arrive at Hong Kong for instructions only, and proceed up the river at once, or to an opium station some forty miles from Hong Kong . . . Hong Kong has really no redeeming point at this moment. The little trade that existed from 1843 to 1847 has gradually become dissolved. There is no inducement for the Chinese to bring produce there, or to settle for the purpose of trade.'[27] These statements were certainly overstating the case, although they found justification in the fact that Hong Kong was a heavy burden on the home Government. They missed the point that this was a period when adjustments were being made to the entirely new treaty-port system, when confidence was gradually increasing, and when commercial links and services were being integrated. Another explanation of the prevailing pessimistic view was the disappointment of the British merchants by the China market for British manufactures. The exports of British manufactures to China were less in value by over half a million dollars in 1850 than in 1844. The common expectation had been that, while other foreign countries could trade only to the five treaty ports, the Chinese could trade anywhere in their junks from Hong Kong, and that they would thus make it the chief centre for Chinese foreign trade. The British merchants did not know, however, that in the Chinese text of the Treaty there was a stipulation forbidding this which was strictly enforced by the Chinese authorities in Canton. As a result, no trade of this type developed, and the port of Hong Kong was fully utilized only by the smuggling trade.

Exact statistics of this illegal traffic were not kept, but exports from India and other sources show that the Chinese consumption of opium increased from 28,508 chests in 1842 to 43,075 chests in 1849. In 1850, a memorandum to the Governor stated that fully three-fourths of the entire Indian opium crops from 1845 to 1849 were deposited at and reshipped from Hong Kong. Most foreign ships trading with China called at Hong Kong or Macao[28] to discharge their illicit cargo and then went straight on to Shanghai, Tientsin and Ningpo to pursue their proper trade. Chinese goods were shipped directly from Shanghai and Canton, by-passing Hong Kong on the return journey. The tendency for foreign ships to go up the Pearl River to Whampoa was still strong because of the ship-repairing service there. Hong Kong had no docking facilities until the Lamont Dock in Aberdeen was completed in 1857. Lorchas[29] under Hong Kong and Macao register were engaged everywhere up and down the China coast, taking advantage of the foreign registry. The *Arrow* was one such smuggling vessel, whose arrest by the Canton authorities led to the Arrow War of 1857–8 and the subsequent cession of the Kowloon peninsula and Stonecutters Island in 1860. However damaging this smuggling trade was to the reputation of the Colony, it was a fact that the Colony benefited indirectly from an increase in the shipping which used the port, while much wealth was accumulated by the firms in this trade.

Despite the importance of the opium traffic to the development of the port, legitimate trade still played a part although, in the absence of trade figures, its share cannot be evaluated. Shipping records reflect the growth of trade: 672 vessels of 226,998 tons arrived at the port in 1845 compared with 884 vessels of 299,009 tons in 1850.[30] Apart from raw cotton and yarn, shirtings, woollens, metals and Straits produce like pepper and rattan, cargoes imported were highly miscellaneous. British manufactures including textiles, Indian cotton and cotton yarn, entered mainly through the entrepôt trade, being redistributed to Shanghai, Amoy and Canton. Exports from Hong Kong were Chinese goods: tea, silk, porcelain, mattings, sugar, indigo and a variety of curiosities. The hinterland of the port could only be broadly indicated as the China coast and South China. There are no means of telling the final destination of such cargo as opium or the origin of the 'treasure' (silver coins) which was exported in payment for the opium. Ships loaded in Hong Kong went to England, Bombay, Madras, Calcutta, Singapore, Sydney, Mauritius, Boston, New York, South America and the East Indian Archipelago.

After 1850, economic conditions in Hong Kong took a turn for the better and the trade became more diversified. The trade in Canton was carried on increasingly by river steamers from Hong Kong and less by sailing-vessels from abroad. The steamer service offered swifter transport, but one of its great attractions was the insurance service, which covered cargoes on steamers but not on sailing-junks. The safety factor undoubtedly entered into the choice of transport at a time when piracy raged around the port. The trans-Pacific trade was given a sudden spur by the discovery of gold in California. This attraction abroad, together with the unrest in China brought about by the Tai P'ing Rebellion (1852–64), caused a wave of Chinese emigrants to pass through Hong Kong. In June 1853, the Governor reported that in the previous year, 'no less than 30,000 Chinese embarked hence for San Francisco, whose passage money, at the rate of $50 per head, would give a sum of $1,500,000 to ship owners and consignees resident at Hong Kong.'[31] These figures were probably exaggerated as records of the following years show emigrants totalling only 14,000 to 15,000 a year. A large number of emigrants, however, also went to Australia and the East Indies. There is no doubt about the stimulus this traffic gave to shipping and trade in Hong Kong. The emigrant Chinese gave rise to a demand for Chinese goods and provisions on the other side of the Pacific Ocean, and ships were loaded in Hong Kong with cargoes of household goods, from stoves to stools, and of foodstuffs, ranging from rice to ginger. The Harbour Master first reported ships clearing the port for San Francisco in 1849. The number of vessels so recorded rose from twenty-three in 1849 to thirty-four in 1852.

The Tai P'ing Rebellion caused the first sudden increase of population in Hong Kong. From a total of 39,017 in 1853, numbers rose to 55,715 in 1854, and to 72,607 in 1855. The port had a brief period of busy activity when the junk trade of Canton migrated to Hong Kong to get away from the disturbance, and when smuggling was facilitated by the general paralysis of the Chinese Imperial Customs Service. This was followed by a fall in trade, however, when the Rebellion spread to the tea and silk-producing areas in the Yangtze provinces, and when the Arrow War and the destruction of the Canton factories interrupted the movement of cargoes.

The Arrow War not only led to the physical expansion of the port, by the addition of part of the Kowloon peninsula and Stonecutters Island, but also to the transfer of the headquarters of foreign trade from Canton to Hong Kong. The transformation of Canton from the only port of China's foreign trade to a mere outpost for the port of Hong Kong was thus completed. Of great importance to the development of the port of Hong Kong was the fact that the whole of the western part of the harbour was now brought under British administration. Before the cession of Kowloon, it had not been possible to bring the shipping in the harbour under effective control. The arrangements with the Chinese authorities had been that it would be regarded as neutral. The

opportunities for fraud and disorder were infinite and the lack of
incentive for improving the port facilities in such conditions has already
been referred to.

A sharp rise in the population figure in 1860–1, to a total of 119,321,
was largely the result of the inclusion of the Kowloon figures but, even
before cession was effected, Chinese people fleeing from unrest and war
began to move in. After 1861, the increase was almost negligible; the
actual figures, changing within one to four thousands, have little significance when the movement of people in and out of the Colony was in
the range of six to twelve thousands a year.

As the population increased, commercial and shipping links were
gradually extended beyond the immediate neighbourhood of the port.
Of notable importance was the progress in shipping connections with
Japan, the Philippines and Siam. Evidence of the growth of commercial
interests was given by the formation of the General Chamber of Commerce in 1861 as the need grew for a united effort 'to watch over and
protect the general interests of commerce.'[32] The important role played
by the commercial and, later, the industrial community in the development of the port was clearly indicated by their influence on government
policy from an early date. Within the first decade of its formation, the
Chamber urged the expansion of trade by government action. Among
the demands in the memorandum addressed to the Secretary for the
Colonies in 1867 were: to secure permission for vessels to ply on the
Yangtze and for the extension of steamboat traffic in the Canton River;
for the right of residence at other places than the treaty ports, and for
extending facilities of trade into the interior markets and along the coast.
These suggestions provided a useful guide to the home Government
when negotiations opened with the Chinese Government in 1897.

The economic development of the port received a slight setback during
1866 when business was affected by the trade depresson in China. The
purchasing power of China was crippled by the destruction caused by
the Rebellion. As Hong Kong was the distribution centre for foreign
imports into China, its trade suffered too. At the same time, obstruction
to the junk trade using the port was caused by the Canton authorities,
who set up customs stations immediately outside the harbour limit,
at Foo-tow-moon, Kap Shui Mun and Cheung Chau. Armed steam
launches covered all the approaches to the harbour and interfered
with all junks entering or leaving the harbour. This 'blockade of the
port', as it was generally called, was continued for nineteen years,
until 1886.

The effects of the depression and the blockade were soon obviated by two major events in the development of communications: the opening of the Suez Canal in 1869 and the completion of a through-telegraph cable from Shanghai and Hong Kong to Europe in 1871. The opening of the Canal was to emphasize the importance of speed in shipping and hence in cargo handling in the port. It also led to the decline in the use of sailing-vessels and to the more general use of iron hulls. The size of the steamers trading along the China coast steadily increased from an average of 670 tons in 1872 to 845 tons in 1881. Sailing-vessels continued for a time, but in diminishing numbers, to carry cargo to Japan and to Australia. Anchorages in Macao and Whampoa gradually fell into disuse.

A change in the method of conducting business was brought about by the telegraph. There was less freedom for merchant firms and they now assumed the position of agent houses executing orders from manufacturers in Europe. There was also less opportunity for speculation as market reports were easily distributed. Business firms could dispense with the keeping of heavy stocks, which meant that small importers and exporters could share the trade with the larger firms.

The two decades following the opening of the Suez Canal were a period of steady progress in the Colony. The population figures, which had almost stagnated since the drop in 1866, were again on the increase after 1872, and kept rising until 1890. Peace was generally maintained in China but famines in 1876 and 1877 sent people to Hong Kong. In response to the growing demand for accommodation in the Colony, land values rose by 15% to 50% in 1881. The period also saw the beginning of the acceptance of foreign manufactured goods by the Chinese, and Hong Kong took an increasing share in China's trade, which was largely a trade with the British Empire. Figure 9 shows this increase rising sharply in 1887, and it was maintained above the 40% level up to the end of the period. The improvement in trade was relative as well as absolute since the foreign trade of China was rising continuously during the last two decades of the nineteenth century.[33] There was also an increase in the diversification of commodities in Hong Kong's trade. Among the imports passing into China were kerosene, oil, matches, rice, coal, dye, tin-plate, lead and iron; among the exports were bean and bean-cake, hides and skins, wool, vegetable oil, seeds, straw braid, hemp, tobacco and matting. As most of these commodities were bulky, it is evident that their entry into foreign trade was only made possible by the lower freight rates after the opening of the Suez Canal.

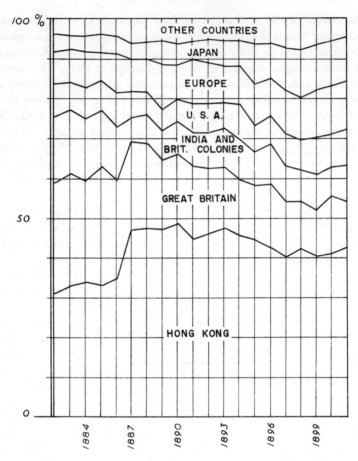

Figure 9. Percentage distribution of China's foreign trade,
1882–1901 (from Banister, 1932, p. 175).

A special feature in the economic development of Hong Kong during
this period was the widening scope of local industries. This meant the
growth of a new line of economic activity, placing demands on services,
facilities and, above all, space. The increasingly important role industry
played was given official acknowledgement by the Governor, Des Voeux,
who reported to Lord Knutsford in October 1889: 'While commerce
pure and simple is, and must be for a long time to come, the principal
element of our prosperity, it is, I think, from manufacture that may be
hoped the greatest progress of Hong Kong in the future.'[34] In the purely

entrepôt economy, all effort tended to concentrate on commerce and shipping. All that was done to the imported goods was the breaking down of bulk, re-packing and re-labelling. The earlier industries such as shipbuilding and ship-repairing, and rope manufacturing were to serve the shipping business. The other industries that existed were mainly food processing: the preparation of preserved ginger, soy-making, sugar-refining, and distilling. But, in the 1880s, a variety of manu-facturing industries were started: the manufacture of cigars and tobacco, glass and umbrellas, weaving and dyeing, iron-founding and tanning, as well as a wide range of arts and crafts. Industrial development was not under any form of government control nor did it receive any official encouragement. The major reason for its growth was the incessant supply of labourers, craftsmen and capital from China, all in search of profitable employment. To a certain extent, the new industries were congruous with the trade that passed through the port. Since Chinese goods for re-export lacked uniformity in quality, adulteration being not uncommon, processing preparatory to export was necessary. Some materials were more profitable to export in the semi-manufactured form. The transhipment point, with its plentiful supply of cheap labour, was obviously the right place for such processes. Weaving and dyeing, tanning, cigar and tobacco manufacture were typical of work carried out to up-grade the value of the export trade.

At the end of the nineteenth century, great changes were taking place in the economic and political outlook of China, with repercussions on Hong Kong. The rush for concessions and 'spheres of influence' by foreign powers, which started about 1885, culminated in the Sino-Japanese War of 1894–5. The defeat by Japan, the then young and small industrial neighbour, awakened the Chinese people to the importance of industrial development. The privilege granted to foreigners to erect and operate factories in the treaty ports of China, the opening of China's inland waterways to navigation by foreign vessels, and the construction of railways by foreign concessions all led to changes in China's foreign trade. This, in turn, demanded considerable adjustment in Hong Kong, still its greatest partner in trade. With its territory greatly expanded by the lease of the New Territories in 1898 and through the opening of the Chinese market, by the end of the nineteenth century Hong Kong had become a prosperous colony.

CHAPTER THREE

DEVELOPMENT PRIOR TO THE
SECOND WORLD WAR

TOWARDS the end of the nineteenth century, Hong Kong's position as a major port in world trade and as a terminus for China's coastal trade was firmly established. Since land transport in China was practically undeveloped, an efficient link between its coastal and inland waterways and the world shipping routes was vital to its economic development. Hong Kong with its transhipment facilities and commercial services provided such a link, while the port itself flourished with the gains of the entrepôt trade.

The extent to which commercial relationships developed between Hong Kong and China can be gauged from the facts that, in the year 1900, 41% of China's foreign trade passed through Hong Kong and that China's share in Hong Kong's foreign trade was 33%.[1] As evidence of the expanding shipping activity in the port, the tonnage of ships entered and cleared doubled in 15 years, to reach the figure of 14 millions in 1900. British shipping interests still had a long lead both in Hong Kong and in the open ports of China, being 65% and 59% respectively.

The bulk of the coasting trade was in the hands of two concerns, the China Navigation Co. (Butterfield and Swire Ltd. in Hong Kong), and the Indo-China Steam Navigation Co. (Jardine Matheson and Co. Ltd. in Hong Kong). Other major coastal shipping interests were the Canton and Macao Steamship Co. and the Douglas Steamship Co. Among the companies that operated inter-ocean shipping in Hong Kong were the Peninsular and Oriental, the Blue Funnel Line, the Glen Line, the Canadian Pacific, and the Bank Line. At this time, when sailing-ships had been almost completely displaced from the South China Sea,[2] the demand for keeping to timetables and schedules became the rule rather than the exception. The maintenance of schedules was greatly facilitated by the extensive network of feeder services furnished by coastal and inland shipping.

The local Chinese firms with branches in China were of tremendous value to the expansion of the entrepôt trade. The Chinese written language was a great hindrance to direct dealings between Chinese traders and merchants and manufacturers in foreign countries. Trade was conducted by British and other foreign import and export firms who had direct contact with the Chinese merchants established in Hong Kong, purchasing from them the produce of China which had been assembled from all parts of the country. The Chinese firms provided a useful means of ensuring deliveries in accordance with sample, as well as of providing information on the changing demands of the Chinese market. Foreign goods were sold to Chinese traders who passed them on to dealers and shopkeepers in the interior.

In view of the heavy dependence of Hong Kong on the China trade, it is evident that economic and political changes in China often demanded adjustments in Hong Kong. At the close of the nineteenth century, China entered a period of active industrial development and railway construction. This was largely the result of foreign investment and the realization by the Chinese of the importance of internal communications during the Sino-Japanese War of 1894–5. By the Treaty of Shimonoseki, privilege was granted to foreigners to erect and operate factories in the treaty ports of China. The first such factories were cotton and silk mills, followed by factories for wool, flour, cement, tobacco, matches and vegetable-oil extraction. The demand for cotton and cotton yarn increased. Great Britain continued to be the chief supplier of cotton manufactures up to the year 1914, after which its place was taken by Japan. A demand also grew for industrial and railway equipment, mainly textile and electrical machinery and materials for railway construction from Great Britain, Japan, the U.S.A. and Germany. There was a marked expansion in China's trade in miscellaneous products, such as the import of kerosene, coal, sugar, rice, dyes and tin-plate, and the export of skins, seeds, bean and bean-cake, wool, hemp, egg and egg products, tobacco and matting. To a certain extent the growth in the export of miscellaneous products resulted from the development of the railways, which opened up new areas of supply.

The rapid rise in Japanese activities in China greatly altered Hong Kong's role in China's foreign trade. The victory of the Japanese in the War of 1894–5 gave them immense opportunities for developing North China. Japanese manufactures competed freely in the China market with other foreign produce. Their activities led to an increase in the export of food products, especially bean and bean products, and the development of such North-China ports as Tientsin and Dairen. With the transport facilities in China improved as a result of the expansion of the railway system, ship owners showed much more readiness to send their ocean steamers to ports which had hardly been heard of before. The tendency for large concentrations of transhipment in Hong Kong and in Shanghai weakened, and the dispersal of port activities became marked. Hong Kong recorded reductions in the entrepôt trade in flour from the Pacific coast of North America (1908), in rice from Saigon (1909), in sugar from Java (1910), and in coal from Japan and French Indo-China (1911), as direct shipments were made from these countries to China. A falling trend in Hong Kong's share in the China trade, which continued until the outbreak of the second Sino-Japanese War in 1937, was firmly established in the early years of the twentieth century (Fig. 10).

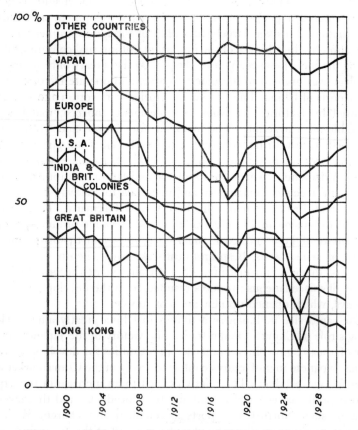

Figure 10. Percentage distribution of China's foreign trade, 1898–1931 (from Banister, 1932, p. 175).

As an entrepôt between the United Kingdom and China, Hong Kong's position also declined. As late as 1889, nearly half the United Kingdom's exports to China passed through Hong Kong. After 1889, this proportion gradually decreased until, for the period 1904–13, the average was only 22% (Table 2).

TABLE 2. HONG KONG AS ENTREPÔT FOR GREAT BRITAIN'S TRADE WITH CHINA (AVERAGE ANNUAL VALUE)

	1890–3 £ thousands	*1894–1903* £ thousands	*1904–13* £ thousands
Imports from China	4,505	2,784	4,011
Imports from Hong Kong	1,012	726	580
Exports to China	5,956	6,066	11,131
Exports to Hong Kong	2,095	2,419	3,594

SOURCE: Gull, E.M., 1943, p. 52.

A comparison of the figures for the United Kingdom exports to China and exports to Hong Kong shows a decline in the relative position of Hong Kong, although actual values were increasing. As the foreign trade of Hong Kong was increasing continuously during these years, the fall in the relative importance of China and the United Kingdom indicates that Hong Kong's trade was becoming more world-wide. This development proved to be timely in view of the prospect of further reductions in the China trade. As the twentieth century advanced, Hong Kong faced greater and greater threats to its economic development from the growth of economic nationalism in China.

Physical Development

At the close of the nineteenth century, Hong Kong was afforded the greatest physical expansion in its history as a result of the leasing from the Chinese Government of the New Territories, an area of 355 square miles. This extension of the area of the Colony was claimed to meet the threat to British interests in South China by French activities in Kwang-chow Wan. The prime object of the lease was the strengthening of the defence of the Colony, although the need to relieve overcrowding on the Island must have been a consideration. Of great significance to the development of the port was the fact that, by pushing the frontier some fifteen miles further to the north, Kowloon was brought into the centre of the Colony, and the entirety of the harbour was restored. Before this change, Kowloon was on the periphery of the Colony, and much useful land was devoted to military occupation. Now development on the peninsula could proceed with a view to integration and co-ordination with that in Victoria and, as early as 1902, a bridge link between the Island and the mainland was advocated by the Harbour Master.[3] Although this proposal has never been acted on it has been revived repeatedly, as, for example, in 1956.[4] Kowloon entered a period of phenomenal growth from the beginning of the twentieth century, and the port developed, embracing the harbour and the twin cities of Victoria and Kowloon. The harbour limit was extended eastwards from North Point to Lei Yue Mun and westwards from Sham Shui Po to Lai Chi Kok (Fig. 11). This made the whole of Kowloon Bay and the sheltered waters north-east of Stonecutters Island available for future port development. The physical barrier of the Kowloon range of hills was then the only limit to urban development. Between the hills and Boundary Street, the pre-1898 boundary, an area of seven and a half square miles, known as New Kowloon, was made available for housing, recreation and other purposes.

Before the end of the nineteenth century, the coastline to the west of the peninsula had been completely modified (Fig. 8). Two major areas were reclaimed from shallow water: Yau Ma Tei and Tai Kok Tsui. Another large scheme started in 1916 was the Kowloon Bay reclamation by the Kai Tak Land Investment Company, a Chinese syndicate, for the purpose of making a residential district for the Chinese. This project involved 210 acres of land, of which 151 were to be reclaimed from shallow water. However, the scheme made little progress after 1921 and was resumed by the Government in 1927 for the development of Kai Tak airport. Other reclamations were carried out by the dock company and the Green Island Cement Company at Hung Hom, and by private enterprise at Ma Tau Kok.[5] In the first two decades of the present century, further, extensive reclamations took place in all parts of the peninsula. Figure 11 summarizes the coastal changes in these years, showing the location and extent of the reclamations. The degree of development might be more accurately gauged if the volume of the fill for these reclamations could be measured. Most of it was obtained from the levelling and cutting of hills to provide building land and through roads.

On the Island, the final stages of change in the coastline during the pre-1941 period were brought about by the Praya East Reclamation and the reclamation at North Point. The Praya East Reclamation Scheme was considered by an eminent merchant, Paul Chater, as early as 1897,

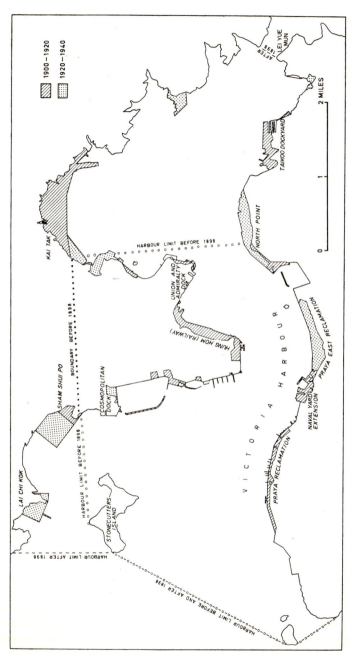

Figure 11. Reclamation in Hong Kong Island and Kowloon, 1900–40.

but it was not until 1921 that it was sanctioned by the Government. One of the major difficulties was that of securing an agreement between the marine lot holders and the Government: the latter intended to be no more than 'one of the interested parties'[6] in the scheme. Another obstacle to the early implementation of the scheme was the inadequate water supply obtainable on the Island, since this would be yet further taxed by a large-scale development of residential areas. The final solution to this problem was found in the laying of a cross-harbour pipeline which began to supply the Island with water from the New Territories in 1930, the year in which the Praya East Reclamation was completed. It is interesting to note that over one-third of the land reclaimed was given over to the construction of streets, the participants shared among them only 60% of the land.

At North Point, reclamation was completed in 1934. Both areas were quickly developed for residential purposes along lines laid down by the Town Planning Committee.[7]

At Kowloon, the irregular shape of the original coastline continued to be smoothed over as land was extended into areas of shallow water. Most of this extension was carried out at the northern fringe of the harbour, at Sham Shui Po, Cheung Sha Wan and Ma Tau Kok. On the eastern shore of Kowloon Bay, the only development was the reclamation intended for the bunkering installations of the Shell Oil Company. Before the Pacific War, this part of New Kowloon had not been brought into the scope of urban development and yet, as in many other parts inside the harbour area, the first development it received came from the shipping services of the port.

The history of reclamation outlined above and in the previous chapter shows that reclamation as a means of meeting the ever-increasing demand for land has been a continuous practice since the founding of the Colony. Reclaimed land is expensive, yet it has been sustained by financial inducement in that the value of the land reclaimed has always exceeded the cost, as the Praya Reclamation of 1889–1904 and the Praya East Reclamation of 1921–30, two of the biggest schemes on the Island, bear witness.[8]

The acquisition of the Kowloon peninsula and the lease of the New Territories, however, provided many level sites for building. There seemed to be unbalanced development when a frenzy of reclamation continued while stretches of level ground inland remained untouched. Murray Rumsey, the Harbour Master, urged in 1903 that instead of providing further space for the increasing population by means of reclamation from the water area, already insufficient for the needs of shipping, all reclamation at or about the harbour frontage should be prohibited, and Kowloon and the New Territories utilized and developed.[9] This view was endorsed by the succeeding Harbour Master, B. Taylor, in 1904.[10] The object, as proposed by these two who represented official interests in the well-being of the port, was threefold, namely, the conservation of berthing accommodation in the harbour, the development of land already available in Kowloon and the New Territories, and the provision of a cross-harbour road link.

In view of the very extensive reclamations since completed, and of the continued efficient handling of shipping in the harbour, it is certain that the fear of land encroachment on the water space in Victoria harbour was premature in 1903. Except for the Praya Reclamation on the Island, then near completion, the reclamations were carried out in areas of shallow water which could not be used by ships of substantial size. By bringing land to the verge of deep water, reclamation actually improved the usefulness of the foreshore. It also eliminated the stretches of noxious tidal flats that fringed all the re-entrants in the coastline, especially in Tai Kok Tsui, Yau Ma Tei, Sham Shui Po and Kowloon Bay.

The preference of entrepreneurs for developing water sites rather than land sites reflects the need for water transport in a period when motor traffic on roads did not exist, as well as the importance of a linkage between the old town of Victoria and rapidly-developing Kowloon. There was only one public ferry operating a regular service between Ice House Street on the Island and the Kowloon godown wharf. Communication between the Island and other districts of Kowloon was maintained by small launches, some of which stopped at places along the waterfront looking for passengers. No regular pier was available for these services. As evidence of the busy cross-harbour traffic, the number of passengers was reported as not less than 6 million annually[11] at a time when the population figure was only 198,964 in Hong Kong Island and Kowloon, including 17,243 in New Kowloon.[12] The proposal in 1903 for the construction of a cross-harbour bridge, before the full development of ferry services, represented tremendous foresight in providing for the growth of internal communications and for the integration of urban services on both sides of the harbour. Unfortunately the scheme was never carried out.

Continued prosperity in the entrepôt trade and expansion in shipping activities demanded improvements in port facilities. Increasing difficulties in providing berthing accommodation for ocean-going steamers were reported in 1901 and 1903. The last decade of the nineteenth century also saw a large increase in the number and size of men-of-war in Hong Kong harbour, occasioned by the Boxer Rebellion in China and the scramble for concessions; the French expansion in Tongking; and the Spanish-American war over the Philippines. The demand for repair services outgrew the docking facilities of the Hong Kong and Whampoa Dock Company, which already owned five docks. Many vessels were compelled to seek repair service at other ports. In an attempt to meet this demand, the Company prepared for the construction of another, bigger, dry dock in 1897. The project met with tremendous opposition from the Company's shareholders and from the Admiralty authorities. The former took into consideration the fact that a new docking company was already building a larger dock, while the Admiralty had then in hand a naval dockyard extension scheme of considerable magnitude. There was grave fear of a fall in the demand for docking services when peace was restored, and the project did not go through. In the year 1908, the new dock company—the Taikoo Dockyard and Engineering Company Ltd.—completed in Quarry Bay (Fig. 11) one of the most up-to-date shipbuilding and ship-repairing works in the Far East. When designed in 1900, its graving-dock was capable of accommodating the largest ship then afloat, the *Oceanic,* 685 ft. 8 in. in length and with a 68 ft. 4 in. beam. Built on fifty-two and a half acres of land, part of which was reclaimed from the sea and part cut out of solid rock, the dockyard occupies an ideal position as it is situated immediately inside Lei Yue Mun Pass, the deep-water entrance to the harbour, with deep water alongside.

Started at about the same time as the Taikoo Dockyard construction, the naval dockyard (Fig. 11) extension was completed two years earlier, in 1906. It consisted of a large dry dock and a tidal basin with deep-water berths alongside the breakwater. The decision to carry out this extension was no doubt induced by tension in the Far East. The commercial community of the Colony, on the other hand, viewed the expansion with misgiving and took the opportunity to petition the home Government for the removal of the naval yard, which cut the praya in two, and confined traffic to a single narrow road.[13] It was also argued that unless this obstruction was removed, the natural expansion of the city would be irretrievably ruined as, owing to the configuration of the ground, it was the only possible direction in which expansion could take place. The petition, endorsed by Sir Henry Blake, the Governor, was unsuccessful and the naval establishment became strongly entrenched in the heart of the city, after its extension was finished.

The completion of these two large dockyards marked the peak as well as the conclusion of the development of docking facilities in Hong Kong. There was no dry-dock construction after 1908. A number of shipbuilding yards have, however, grown up since, under Chinese management. These are scattered along the shore at Tai Kok Tsui, Cheung Sha Wan and north-east Kowloon Bay, and are engaged in the building and repairing of light craft. The naval dockyard dealt solely with the maintenance of naval vessels, but the two commercial dockyards, the Hong Kong and Whampoa Dock Co. and the Taikoo Dockyard and Engineering Co. Ltd., have long been familiar to all associated with shipping in the Far East. The importance of their efficient ship maintenance and repair service, at a point where the major shipping routes cross the most frequented typhoon tracks of the Far East, is evident. In the economic development of the Colony, the dockyards have played an important role as the leading heavy industry, employing a total of 12,000 workers in an average year.

TABLE 3. DEEP-WATER BERTHS IN HONG KONG HARBOUR, 1925

Location	Maximum draught of vessel which may berth alongside at L.W.O.S.T.	Number of vessels which may berth simultaneously
HONG KONG ISLAND		
China Merchant's pier and Jardine's Wharf (West Point)	23 ft.	3
Douglas pier (Central)	26 ft.	2
Ching Sion Land Investment Co.'s Wharfs (North Point)	28 ft.	3
KOWLOON		
Hong Kong and Kowloon Wharf and Godown Co.'s piers and Holt's Wharf	25 ft.	4
	28 ft.	2
	30 ft.	2
	32 ft.	2
	Total	18

SOURCE: Hong Kong Port Development Department, *Report of the Commercial Development of the Port of Hong Kong,* by J. Duncan, 1924.

The shortage of berthing accommodation in the harbour was overcome with similar vigour, during the first quarter of this century. While building the new dockyard at Quarry Bay, the firm of Butterfield and

Swire, representing the interests of the Blue Funnel Line on the China coast, started to develop the deep-water frontage at Kowloon Point, in 1906. The development consisted of deep-water wharves, cargo sheds and warehouses, collectively known as Holt's Wharf. In 1915, the Hong Kong and Kowloon Wharf and Godown Co. extended their warehouses and completed another pier for ocean-going steamers. Approaches to the piers were dredged. Another site at North Point was developed for deep-water berths by a private investor in 1924, so that, by 1925, there were eighteen berths for vessels of deep draught.

Parallel with the increase in shipping engaged in foreign trade, there was an increase in the number of small craft directly or indirectly employed in the transhipment service. Accommodation for these craft was a growing problem in the early years of the century. Shelter for junks and sampans was necessary not only during the passage of typhoons but also at times of strong monsoon. The typhoon refuge at Causeway Bay was grossly inadequate, and the need to provide more protection for small craft in the harbour was repeatedly urged by the business community.[14] However, shelter for small craft had to be provided by the Government, since it could not be made a commercial proposition. More than 3,000 craft of all sizes and over 3,000 lives had been lost in typhoons between 1900 and 1908[15] before work was started on the Mong Kok shelter. Completed in 1915, it enclosed an area of 165 acres and has since remained a prominent feature of the harbour. Situated to the leeward of the peninsula and close to the moorings where most cargoes were discharged or loaded, it proved more useful than the old shelter at Causeway Bay. This is because strong winds in Hong Kong usually come from the easterly quarter and the majority[16] of gales first set in from the north-east quadrant. For native craft entirely dependent on sails and oars, it is hazardous to try to reach the Causeway Bay shelter from the western part of the harbour after the wind has risen.

The improvements in ocean-going steamer accommodation during this period, although enormous in themselves, still left a gap between demand and supply. John Duncan, the Port Engineer, in 1924 estimated a daily average of seventy vessels in port, half of which would require wharfage accommodation.[17] The demand was thus only half met. The long-sustained practice of overside discharge and loading midstream was found unsuitable for the most economic handling of cargo. The disadvantage of relying too heavily on unskilled labour in the transhipment service became more pronounced as national feeling grew among the Chinese. Strikes, boycotts and an exodus in the 1920s were bitter experiences to those whose interest it was to maintain the unimpeded turn-round of shipping. Stevedoring for vessels anchored midstream was also subject to delays due more to the fear of bad weather during the typhoon season, than to actual rough weather. Warnings were given of typhoons within a 400-mile radius from Hong Kong, and it was difficult to get lighterage service when the risk of rough weather was present. Among other activities affected were the supply of fuel oil and fresh water, and the embarkation of passengers, because the launches which provided these services were put out of operation on the approach of a typhoon. Such inconveniences could have been eliminated if the ships had been berthed at wharves instead of anchored midstream.

Another problem that emerged during this period was that of traffic congestion in the harbour. In 1919, new regular ferry services from various points on the city front of Victoria to Yau Ma Tei, Mong Kok and Sham Shui Po were inaugurated, and since then there has been a gradual increase in the number of ferries employed and in the frequency of service. New routes were opened between Kowloon City, Hung Hom and Shau Kei Wan in 1928, and between Jubilee Street in central Victoria and Jordan Road in Kowloon in 1932. In addition to these, there were numerous private and public utility launches, junks and sampans traversing the harbour in all directions. In the harbour, the movement of coastal and ocean-going steamers engaged in foreign trade was essentially aligned in an east-west direction, as governed by the position of the entrances to the harbour, the quarantine anchorage and the arrangement of the mooring-buoys (Fig. 12). Local traffic by ferries,

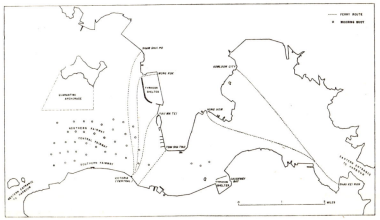

Figure 12. Cross-harbour routes and location of berths and anchorages, 1938.

launches and junks, on the other hand, was mainly north-south. The tendency was for local traffic to increase with the growth of population and coastal and ocean shipping.

It was thus clear that great advantages could be gained by the construction of more piers for the berthing of coasters and ocean-going vessels, since this would take away some of the traffic from inside the harbour and reduce the need for lighterage and other services. Duncan's report on the development of the port, in 1924, recommended a large-scale development of the shore at North Point, Hung Hom, Kowloon Point and Wan Chai. Many of his recommendations revived the views of an earlier report by the consulting engineers to the Crown Agent.[18] The recommendations, however, were never put into effect, as changing economic conditions made the investment of large sums on the development of port facilities inopportune. Between 1925 and the Pacific War, the only addition to the berthage for ocean-going vessels was the 800 ft. wharf completed by the Hong Kong and Kowloon Wharf and Godown Co. in 1932. The main cause of this stagnation in the construction of port works was the trade recession. As Table 4 shows, Duncan's report in 1924 coincided with the peak year of the port's shipping tonnage. From then on there was a steady decline in the volume of traffic in the port as a result of unrest in China, world depression, war between China and Japan and the Second World War.

TABLE 4. SHIPPING IN THE PORT OF HONG KONG, 1919–39

Year	Ocean-going tonnage	Other than ocean-going	Total
1919	14,467,847	21,147,322	35,615,169
1924	27,874,830	28,856,247	56,731,077
1929	28,285,741	18,900,440	47,186,181
1934	28,905,526	13,008,496	41,914,022
1939	22,148,228	8,749,720	30,897,948

SOURCE: Owen, Sir David, *Future Control and Development of the Port of Hong Kong*, 1941.

The policy of the Hong Kong Government towards the lease of pier sites was a contributory cause in discouraging wharf construction. By the Piers Ordinance of 1899, all leases of pier sites were to expire by the end of 1949, after which year the Government would take possession of all piers. There was no condition in the leases giving the lessees the right to, or any expection of, a renewal. The Government's intention was to obtain a free hand in developing the waterfront along systematic lines. Many pier owners were under the impression that their lease would not be renewed, although this was not confirmed by the Government until 13 August 1938. The result was that private interest in pier construction tapered off as the time for which leases could be held shortened.

A period of quiescence in the development of port facilities followed the completion of the 800 ft. wharf at Kowloon Point in 1932. The volume of trade passing through Hong Kong had been on the decline since 1924, as international relations in the Far East and in Europe deteriorated. Judging from the volume of shipping using the port, Sir David Owen, who was invited by the Hong Kong Government to investigate the port facilities and to make recommendations on the future development and control of the port, reported in 1941 that the then existing piers on the Kowloon side of the harbour could provide sufficient accommodation for ocean-going vessels. Piers for coastal and river steamers were, however, described as more or less derelict,[19] and seventeen new piers were recommended for construction at sites along the waterfront of Victoria. No mention was made as to the adequacy of godown facilities, but the warehouses of the Hong Kong and Kowloon Wharf and Godown Co. and of Messrs. Alfred Holt and Co. were regarded as most up-to-date and excellent for their purpose. It was particularly noteworthy that in emphasizing the importance of keeping the port facilities adequate and the burden of its charges as light as possible, Sir David Owen remarked that he was 'struck by the lowness of the charges which the principal godown companies are able to make, they being lower than those at any of the many ports of which I have knowledge.'[20] It is clear that in the period before the Pacific War the development of port facilities in Hong Kong had been well looked after by private enterprise. The existence of derelict piers could be attributed to the fear of government interference with pier rights. There can be no doubt that the situation would have been adequately dealt with if pier owners had been given security of tenure. There is sufficient evidence of the influence of government policy in this sphere in the fact that large-scale developments carried out by the Hong Kong and Kowloon Wharf and Godown Co. were encouraged by the understanding that the administration of their wharves would be given special consideration when all leases of piers expired in 1949.[21]

In the history of the administration of the port is to be found one of the most convincing expressions of the community's preference for the *laissez-faire* attitude of the Government. The administration of the harbour was never run as a separate department. It came within the purview of various officials. The engineering side of the port was a sub-section of the Department of Public Works; the control of navigation within the port was under the Harbour Master, while the Land Department issued the pier leases. There had been no officially-adopted plan of development, although investigations and recommendations were not lacking. All three of the investigating bodies, Messrs Coode, Fitzmaurice and Mitchell, Consulting Engineers to the Crown Agent (1922), John Duncan, the Port Engineer (1924), and Sir David Owen (1941), endorsed the view that private enterprise was in the least favourable position to meet the needs of a growing port and that control by the Government or a Harbour Trust would result in better development. However, such unified control and joint effort in drawing up a planned development has never come into existence.

In the year 1929, the first Harbour Board was formed but without executive power; its function was advisory only. The General Chamber of Commerce was apprehensive that the formation of such a Harbour Board would eventually lead to increased expenses being imposed on shipping. In 1931, the Harbour Board was changed into the Harbour Advisory Committee, a smaller and more flexible body. Ten years later, it was found that this Committee was 'still in existence in name, but no meeting has been held for about two years.'[22] It could not therefore be said to have had much influence on the policy of the port. The recommendation of Sir David Owen to form a public Port Trust or Authority, to take over port management on similar lines to those of the Port of London Authority, was made only shortly before the outbreak of the Pacific War, during which the port came under Japanese military control. Yet after the re-establishment of British rule in Hong Kong in 1946, a Port Administration Inquiry Committee decided against Sir David Owen's recommendation. In place of the Advisory Committee which existed before the War, two advisory committees were created to deal with port affairs: the Port Committee to deal with major present and future problems, and the Port Executive Committee to deal with day-to-day problems. The development of port facilities and their operation still depends on private enterprise.

Population Growth

Hong Kong was at a height of prosperity during the late nineteenth and the early twentieth centuries. From 1897, the Colony financed its own development entirely from local revenue, with the exception of a small loan raised in 1906 to pay for the cost of the British section of the Canton-Kowloon railway. Out of its own resources it paid for heavy expenditure on waterworks, road extension, land reclamation, public buildings, improvement of the port and the rapid transformation of Kowloon from a suburb of Victoria to a large modern city. These achievements were largely the result of the demands imposed by an ever-increasing immigrant population. Unrest in China never failed to send people flocking into Hong Kong. The Boxer Rising in 1900 started the century's first inflow of Chinese with capital to invest under the protection of the British Government. This was immediately followed by increased land sales and enhanced prices of property in the Colony. The total population rose from 221,441 in 1891 to 300,660 in 1901 and to 456,739 in 1911. The 1901 increase reflects the inclusion of population in the New Territories, but since then the increase in population has been concentrated in the urban areas, in particular Kowloon.

The Chinese Revolution in 1911, which led to the overthrow of the Manchu Dynasty, started another flood of Chinese immigrants to the Colony. Government estimates show that at least 20,000 people arrived within a few weeks during the months of April and May 1911, and the total increase in the population of the Colony as a result of the Revolution was between 40,000 and 50,000.[23] Renewed political unrest in 1913 brought in an estimated 60,000 new immigrants.[24] By far the greater proportion of these refugees came from the near-by provinces of Kwangtung, Kwangsi and Fukien. Though some returned to China as soon as conditions there settled, a considerable number remained, causing a great strain on the housing resources of the Colony. The inflow of Chinese to Hong Kong never stopped during the three decades after the Revolution. Civil war in China continued for twenty years after 1911 and, when a unified government was in sight in the 1930s, Japanese activities in North China provoked open war.

Not all refugees were destitute. Many of them were middle-class artisans or well-to-do merchants seeking a place of security where they could practise their trade without interference and where they could be sure of reaping profit from their investments. The continued building boom after 1912 gave witness to the rich resources of the immigrant Chinese. The following table, showing the number of new houses built in the decade 1910–19, provides a clear picture of the extent and direction of urban growth.

TABLE 5. CONSTRUCTION OF CHINESE HOUSES, 1910–19

Year	City including North Point.	Other parts of Hong Kong	Kowloon	Total
1910	40	19	6	65
1911	72	3	22	97
1912	71	9	43	123
1913	133	12	22	167
1914	88	18	67	173
1915	141	14	77	232
1916	153	10	69	232
1917	133	12	99	244
1918	81	14	150	245
1919	61	4	235	300
Total	973	115	790	1,878

SOURCE: Report of Public Works Committee, 5 February 1920, *Hong Kong Sessional Paper* 1920.

From the above table it can be seen that the rate of house construction on the Island accelerated after the Chinese Revolution but fell off after 1917, as building sites became difficult to obtain, while in Kowloon it started off gradually but accelerated throughout the period.

The higher concentration of property development in Kowloon in the second and third decades of this century can be illustrated by comparing the census figures for the years 1911, 1921 and 1931. The population of Kowloon more than doubled during the decade 1921–31.

TABLE 6. POPULATION OF HONG KONG IN 1911, 1921 AND 1931

	1911	1921		1931	
	Population	Population	Increase percentage	Population	Increase percentage
Island of Hong Kong	244,323	347,401	+42·19%	409,203	+ 17·79%
Kowloon Peninsula	67,497	123,448	+82·96%	263,020	+113·06%
New Territories	80,622	83,163	+ 3·15%	98,157	+ 18·02%
Floating	60,948	71,154	+61·74%	70,093	− 1·49%
Unclassified	3,349	—	—	—	—
Total	456,739	625,166	+36·87%	840,473	+34·44%

SOURCE: *Hong Kong Census Reports*, 1911, 1921, and 1931.

The greatest increase occurred in the new suburban districts of Tai Kok Tsui and Sham Shui Po. A comparison of the rate of increase in Kowloon and in Hong Kong also indicates that the Island had almost reached saturation point. Population density in West Point for the year 1931 was 1,178 per acre while the highest corresponding figure in Kowloon (in Yau Ma Tei) was only 350 per acre. There is no doubt that in the 1920s Kowloon developed partly at the expense of Hong Kong Island. Improved housing accommodation, in the form of the modern ferro-concrete type of buildings being built in Kowloon, was sought by the artisan and middle classes, while the labouring class crowded into West Point to find housing as close as possible to the places of work.

This relatively intensive development in Kowloon is partly explained by the greater availability of building sites and partly by the construction of the railway which linked Kowloon and Canton. The railway provided a much-needed means of communication between the New Territories and the urban districts of Kowloon, and its construction gave rise to many ancillary developments.

The inflow of Chinese people assumed flood proportions again after the outbreak of the Sino-Japanese War in July 1937. An excess of immigrants over emigrants of 100,000 was estimated for the year 1937 and the figure increased to 500,000 in 1938.[25] These estimates included only people arriving by railway and sea; no account could be given of those entering by sampans, junks or across the land frontier on foot. Many of these arrived destitute and an unprecedented problem of food and accommodation arose. Up to 1937, the inflow of Chinese did not affect the rural villages of the New Territories, but later, thousands of immigrants had to crowd into these market towns and villages. Thousands took to living on the sidewalks of streets under verandahs and in shacks erected on vacant pieces of Crown Land. A census taken in June 1938 by the Police Department gave the number of street-sleepers as 270,000.

The fall of Canton to Japanese forces, on 21 October 1938, slowed down the stream of immigrants but did not stop it entirely; people were still coming in through Macao and other towns on the South China coast. In the wake of this flood of poverty-stricken refugees came the inevitable epidemics of infectious diseases. In alleviating the conditions of the refugees, the resources of the government agencies and private charities were so strained that it was considered necessary to tackle the problem at its source. In 1940, immigration control had to be instituted for the first time in the history of the Colony. The operation of immigration control, however, was ineffective and the inflow continued. The

estimated population of the Colony in 1941 was 1,639,337,[26] an increase
of 95% in ten years.

It is evident that an increase of such magnitude was not justified by
the economic position of the Colony in that period. On the other hand,
it was the necessity for absorbing this unnatural and phenomenal
increase that gave rise to much social and economic development.

The Railway

As the first modern method of land transport to connect the port of
Hong Kong with its hinterland, the influence of the Kowloon-Canton
railway on the development of the port needs detailed investigation.
Hong Kong's growth being largely dependent on the China trade, the
Colony's merchants were keenly interested in improving the transport
link with South China. Both the colonial Government and the commercial
community had urged the construction of the Canton-Kowloon railway
since the lease of the New Territories was effected. In the first decade of
the twentieth century, the building of this railway was stimulated by the
scramble for foreign concessions and spheres of influence in China. It
was one small part of the widespread railway development during that
period.[27] However, the vision of Hong Kong's community was that the
port should benefit by a direct through-railway link with the Chinese
national railway system.[28]

A concession for the building of the Canton-Kowloon railway was
obtained by the British and Chinese Corporation in 1898, but for various
reasons the construction work was delayed. The main difficulties were
the provision of funds and the subsequent working of the Chinese
section of the line. It was understood in the preliminary Agreement that
the Chinese Government would not build another line to compete with
this railway. The Chinese Government's proposal to build a line towards
Amoy from Canton provoked much opposition as it was held that such a
line was directly contrary to the Agreement. Without waiting for the
conclusion of the negotiations, the British section of the Kowloon-
Canton railway, twenty-two and a half miles in length, was put in hand
in 1905. Work on the Chinese section, a 90-mile track between Canton
and Shumchun near the border of the Colony, began in 1907, after an
agreement was concluded with the British and Chinese Corporation for
a 5% sterling loan of £1,500,000. Through train traffic was started on
5 October 1911. Northwards from Canton, an international syndicate
was constructing the Canton-Hankow railway as a link between the two
centres of trade. Owing to lack of funds and great engineering difficulties,

work on this line was suspended after 1915. Of the proposed 700-mile track only about 240 miles were completed, running northwards from Canton to Chuchow. In Canton the termini of these two railways—the Canton-Kowloon and the Canton-Hankow—were separated by a distance of only two and a half miles. It is interesting to note that as early as 1910 the Canton-Kowloon railway published a map containing a dotted line drawn from its own terminus at Canton to that of the Canton-Hankow railway. This indicates that a project existed for the connection of the two railways and with it the extension of the hinterland for the port of Hong Kong. In 1922, the British Government decided to remit the balance of the Boxer Indemnity Fund, and strongly urged that the proceeds be used, in part at least, to complete the north-south line running through the heart of South China. Negotiations to effect the through link to Kowloon were taken up long before the railway was finally completed in 1936, and high hopes were expressed that Hong Kong might become the great outlet for the produce of all China south of the Yangtze.

Duncan, on the other hand, basing his hypothesis on an analysis of the nature of the trade of the Colony, held that there was no likelihood whatever of goods from beyond Changsha coming to Hong Kong by rail. He supported his view by pointing out that the depth of water in the Yangtze below Hankow allowed whole year navigation by steamboats; that, except for perishables, the export of raw materials and semi-finished products from the Yangtze provinces could best be transported by ships to Shanghai; assuming that freight rates for one mile of rail haul were equal to those for four miles of water haul, the 'economic divide' for goods going via the Tung Ting Lake and Yangtze to Shanghai, or by rail to Hong Kong, was in the vicinity of Hengyang; and finally that the trade and industry south of this divide, except for silk, were not of sufficient magnitude to affect the export trade of Hong Kong. What Duncan could have added to support his argument was the important fact of growing national feeling in China following the Revolution, which was not congenial to the interests of a port under foreign rule. Although many requests were made to effect the connection of the two lines, interests in Canton were constantly opposed to the proposal. It was feared that direct railway traffic would mean that cargo was not transhipped in Canton, thus reducing the trade passing through Canton. This opposition was strongly held until 1937, when a national emergency made the railway link imperative.

With the completion of the Canton-Hankow railway the importance of Canton as a trading centre increased. While the services rendered to it by the port of Hong Kong were recognized, the need was felt to develop its own national interest. Immediately following the completion of the railway, work began on the redevelopment of the Whampoa harbour to accommodate vessels of 10,000-ton capacity. A twenty-six-mile branch line from the Canton-Hankow railway was extended to the Whampoa harbour in 1937. This was intended to compete with the Canton-Kowloon railway and directly infringed the Agreement of the Canton-Kowloon Railway Loan. However, this development of Whampoa harbour raised no objection from the British Government, not only because the railway to Whampoa harbour provided the long-demanded link between the Canton-Hankow railway and the Canton-Kowloon railway, but also because it was recognized as a necessary measure, the Sino-Japanese War having started in July 1937; and because the roles of the two ports were viewed as complementary and not competitive. Whampoa would serve the commerce between Canton and other ports of China, while Hong Kong would continue to handle international trade.

On 21 October 1938, when the redevelopment of Whampoa harbour had just started and before Hong Kong could suffer any of the consequences of possible competition, Canton and the Pearl River delta area were taken by Japanese forces, putting an end to normal traffic in South China. It had been sufficiently demonstrated, however, that

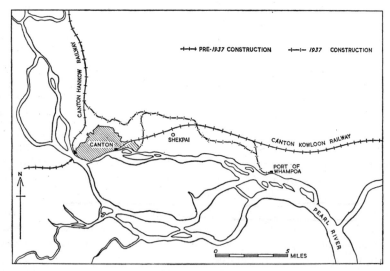

Figure 13. The link between the Canton-Kowloon railway and the Canton-Hankow railway.

nationalism in China was not reconciled to the development of Hong Kong into the principal distribution and collection centre for South China to the detriment of Canton. The linking of the Canton-Hankow railway and the Canton-Kowloon railway was only accepted as 'a logical sequence'[29] to the building of the Canton-Whampoa railway, which could not be done without crossing the Canton-Kowloon railway (Fig. 13). By sanctioning the railway link, the Chinese Government made the best possible provision for the war effort, for Hong Kong became the only large port through which their supplies could pass when the Yangtze River was blocked by war in August 1937. A few months' delay in the joining of the two railways would have meant the loss of several hundred thousand tons of imported military supplies, essential during the early stages of the war.

To the port of Hong Kong, the completion of the Canton-Kowloon railway meant the opening of the first modern land communication with its hinterland. Motorized road traffic did not exist in South China in the early twentieth century. Speed in the transport of goods was the one obvious advantage the railway had over the steamer and junk traffic, yet the small gain in time this new line afforded was insufficient to outweigh the higher freight charges. Moreover, the business centre for the China trade was located within the port of Hong Kong. Nearly all this trade was transacted through Chinese merchant Hongs or firms concentrated in the crowded West Point district of the Island. The warehouses for their cargoes were also on the waterfront of the western part of Victoria. Although the large modern warehouses at Kowloon Point had branches of the railway serving their premises, their storage services were not intended for this trade. Hence goods conveyed by the railway had to be transhipped into lighters or junks in order to reach the warehouses on the Island. This disadvantage considerably reduced the attraction of the railway in competing with steamers and junks. The persistent refusal of the Chinese authorities to effect the railway link to Hankow was a crippling blow to the importance of the Canton-Kowloon railway, as it practically confined the area served by the railway to that which was already well served by river steamers and junks.

As no record was kept of the import of goods from South China, no clear picture of the railway traffic is available. From the figures of Hong Kong's export trade it can be seen that the railway played only a minor role in the transport of goods, as compared with steamers and junks.

TABLE 7. EXPORTS FROM HONG KONG TO SOUTH CHINA, 1918 AND 1919

	1918 *(Value in £ sterling)*	*1919*
Exports from Hong Kong to South China by steamer	12,435,480	13,083,302
Exports from Hong Kong to South China by junk	8,660,870	7,600,220
Exports from Hong Kong to South China by rail	326,193	571,889

SOURCE: Hong Kong, *Trade Returns,* 1918, 1919.

This lack of traffic was hardly expected by the British and Chinese Corporation, which had included in their original design the prevention of competition and the tapping of the South China rail freight. Their plan to make the Kowloon railway station the deep-sea terminus for the South China export trade was not carried through. In any case, the operation of the railway was frequently interrupted, mostly because of unrest and disorder in Kwangtung province. The first interruption came only a month after its inauguration, when the Chinese Revolution broke out. Fighting, robbery, derailment and a collision on the Chinese section continued to disrupt through traffic until 1925, when the passenger stock was in such a bad state of repair that it was considered inadvisable to allow it to run on the British section. Passengers had to change carriages at the international border. After 1927 there was no engine in running order on the Chinese section and the British section provided engines to maintain the whole of the railway for express trains. Haulage charges were paid by the Chinese section from 1927 to 1936, after which year engines were handed over for operation. Internal strife in South China ended in about the same year and Kwangtung underwent a period of extensive road construction. Many new roads were built as feeders to the railway, making it a popular means of transport. Yet it was not long before traffic was disrupted again, by the Japanese occupation of Canton in 1938.

The Boycott

The rise of nationalism in China, which had found expression during the construction of the railway extension to Hong Kong, was also manifested between 1925–6 in the form of a boycott, the major effect of which fell upon the port. The Nationalist movement was widespread in

China after the Revolution of 1911 and strikes and boycotts had been repeatedly directed against foreigners, especially Japanese, since 1905.[30] The boycott of 1925–6 began as an anti-British movement and soon developed almost entirely into a boycott of Hong Kong. It has been pointed out that this boycott of Hong Kong proved to be more effective than any of the preceding ones since the Colony was largely inhabited by Chinese and its main function was that of a distribution and financial centre for all of South China. At the height of the boycott, trade was at a standstill and shipping was seriously hindered. It was estimated that 150,000 Chinese, men, women and children, left Hong Kong within a week. Those who did not leave deserted their posts. The effect of the boycott can best be stated by quoting one of the regulations enforced by the organizations directing the movement: that 'all non-British merchandise and non-British vessels not passing through Hong Kong or Macao shall have freedom of trade.'[31] Similar regulations were applied to Swatow, Foochow, Amoy, Kongmoon, Pakhoi, Wuchow and other ports in Kwangtung, with varying degree of success. Although this boycott was not supported by the Chinese Nationalist Government, it did not end until the Government desired to end it on National Day, 10 October 1926. No trade statistics are available to show the effect of the boycott on trade, but the shipping returns show a sharp decline for these two years.

TABLE 8. SHIPPING IN HONG KONG, 1924–7

| Year | Vessels in foreign trade | | River trade | |
	No.	Tonnage	Imports (tons)	Exports (tons)
1924	57,765	38,770,499	493,711	663,802
1925	41,336	32,179,053	201,128	318,502
1926	30,231	28,371,104	117,421	123,322
1927	51,289	36,834,014	*	*

* Figures not available.
SOURCE: Hong Kong Government, *Annual Reports*, 1924–27.

The number of British steamers entering the harbour of Canton before the boycott varied between 240 and 160 in the months of August and September 1924, but during the corresponding period in 1925 the number varied between twenty-seven and two only.[32] Cargoes were

sent by very circuitous routes to their destinations in China. Goods
in storage in Hong Kong, after all marks on the cases which would
associate them with Hong Kong had been defaced, were conveyed
800 miles north to Shanghai (which was not under the control of
the Nationalist Government) and then shipped south to Canton. In
terms of China's trade, Hong Kong's share fell to just over 10%
and thereafter remained below 20% until the outbreak of the Sino-
Japanese War.

The experience of the boycott underlined two important factors which
not only were a powerful influence on the prosperity of Hong Kong but
which also were entirely outside the Colony's control. The first was
national feeling in China. A friendly relationship with China was
essential as long as Hong Kong remained dependent on the China trade.
The second factor was the need for strong and stable government in the
neighbouring provinces. Although disturbances in South China had
often led to economic expansion in the Colony, Hong Kong could
only establish its trade on a regular footing with a stable Chinese
government.

Shipping Trade and Industry Between the Two World Wars

The worldwide shortage of shipping during the First World War had
repercussions on the trade of Hong Kong. Total tonnage of ships entering and clearing the port dropped from 22,939,134 tons in 1913 to
19,561,318 tons in 1915, and further to 17,329,841 tons in 1917.[33] The
War led to the total withdrawal of all vessels under German and Austrian
flags and to a falling off in large ocean-going vessels from European
ports. Trade with the United Kingdom declined, while the routes across
the Pacific were well supplied by Japanese vessels. Markets which had
formerly taken British goods turned to Japanese goods instead. The
slackening of European competition also provided a chance for China's
industrial expansion. The Chinese market for British goods was not
regained after the War, much to the disadvantage of Hong Kong's
entrepôt trade, since Hong Kong had been the port of entry for British
goods into China. Britain lost her lead in the Chinese trade, being
overtaken first by the Japanese and then by the United States of America.
Hong Kong's share in China's foreign trade further declined to about
25% (Fig. 10), as more direct trade contacts between China, Britain,
Japan and the United States were established. It must be pointed out,
however, that China was still by far the greatest partner in Hong Kong's
trade as the trade returns show (Table 9).

TABLE 9. DIRECTION OF HONG KONG'S FOREIGN TRADE, 1918–20
(VALUE IN £ STERLING)

	1918	*1919*	*1920*
United Kingdom	5,551,604	7,823,105	17,416,102
British Dominion Colonies and Protectorates	15,680,363	24,409,272	28,061,748
China	46,373,189	54,429,396	67,852,063
Japan	14,313,754	19,494,867	16,657,212
Other foreign countries	46,072,067	49,637,324	82,315,414
Total	127,990,977	155,793,964	212,302,539

SOURCE: Hong Kong, *Trade Returns,* 1918, 1919 and 1920.

Recovery from the recession of the boycott period was gradual because political strife in China lessened its purchasing power. China's economic nationalism and continued industrialization led to a decreasing demand for foreign goods. Conditions for trade with China were further worsened in 1929, when China regained her tariff autonomy. Rapid revisions of tariff rates were used by the Chinese Government to foster native industry in order to render the country less dependent on foreign imports, particularly of textiles and foodstuffs. The reduction in China's import trade in relation to the rise of tariffs can be seen from Table 10.

TABLE 10. INDICES OF CHINA'S IMPORT TRADE
AND TARIFF LEVELS, 1926–36

Year	Import quantities	Tariff level
1926	100·0	100·0
1927	82·3	99·8
1928	100·7	100·2
1929	107·2	106·5
1930	98·2	107·6
1931	99·1	111·7
1932	81·3	113·7
1933	79·1	120·5
1934	64·4	129·0
1935	59·6	130·0
1936	55·0	129·2

SOURCE: Cheng Yu-Kwei, *Foreign Trade and Industrial Development of China,* 1956.

Further difficulties for trade arose as the result of the world depression
in the 1930s and the erection of tariff barriers by Southeast Asian
countries, such as the Dutch East Indies, French Indo-China and the
Philippines, which had been important to Hong Kong's trade since the
decline of the trade with China.

Hong Kong's imports in 1933 were valued at £29,000,000 and its
exports at £27,000,000. This was only about 40% of the 1924 value.
There were fewer imports from China and Japan as industry in North
China grew with Japanese investment in China. The increased surtax
on foreign rice imposed by the Canton Government led to fewer rice
cargoes being carried from Bangkok and Saigon to Hong Kong, while
China's policy of growing and refining its own sugar led to reduced
business for the refineries in the Colony. High import duties on coal
caused reductions in coal shipments from Tongking and Borneo. There
was a corresponding decline in shipping visiting the port, and in 1934,
several large factories in the hosiery and knitting trade closed down.
The serious recession in trade is shown in Table 11.

TABLE 11. HONG KONG TOTAL VALUE OF IMPORTS
AND EXPORTS, 1924–33 (IN £ STERLING)

Year	Imports	Exports
1924	72,155,478	63,674,794
1931	34,665,069	28,796,398
1932	36,250,499	30,965,793
1933	29,276,847	27,292,699

SOURCE: Hong Kong, *Report of the Economic Commission,*
1935.

An Economic Commission, appointed in 1934 to investigate the trade
depression in Hong Kong and make recommendations, came to the
conclusion that, unless the entrepôt trade could be developed sufficiently
or alternative markets found to compensate for the loss of entry into
South China, the Colony's rate of growth must slow down. The Commission recognized the necessity for close contacts between Hong Kong
and China and for efforts to work for the mutual benefit of both parties
as well as the fact that, with China increasingly adopting a policy of
economic nationalism, Hong Kong's trade had to change. It was recommended that the Colony be included within the tariff wall of China.

As a result of China's industrial policy, the development of trade must eventually depend on world recovery and on an increase in the ability of China to export.

Industrial Development

One promising development in Hong Kong, stimulated by the 1932 Ottawa Agreement, which emerged after the depression years was the expansion of light industry. Industry had existed in the Colony since the early years of its history but it was not until the twentieth century that light industry began to acquire an important position in its economy. Cotton-spinning, wool-knitting, the making of singlets and shirts and, the manufacture of rattan furniture were the industries introduced in the early 1900s. During the First World War, many goods became difficult to obtain from Europe and factories were set up to supply the local market with biscuits, confectionery, perfumes and cigarettes. After the First World War, Hong Kong manufacturers were faced not only with the return of European competition but also with the growth of protectionism in Asian countries. Yet it was in the 1920s that many new industries were introduced to the Colony, chief among which were the manufacture of leather and rubber-soled footwear, felt hats, electric torches and batteries, and vacuum flasks. A detailed survey by the Economic Commission in 1934 listed a wide variety of light industries in the Colony, with a total capital of $51,244,300.[34] There were 166 factories on the Island and 253 in Kowloon.

Because of the depressed state of world trade and the changes in the Chinese market, the Economic Commission of 1934 was of the opinion that 'the industry of Hong Kong cannot develop much beyond its present stage except in as much as it can form an economic part of the whole industrial development of South China and even to some extent of North China.' However, a definite growth in industry was observed as the effects of the world depression subsided. Most of the existing industries expanded and exports began to absorb a large proportion of their output. Manufactures such as cotton knitwear, rubber footwear and electric torches built up firm markets by taking advantage of Imperial Preference. New industries established during this period were paints, which concentrated from the first on exports to Southeast Asia, and umbrellas. The mid-1930s was a period of consolidation for local industries. Small and speculative investments, unable to stand the test of the difficult years, had closed down. In 1935, there were fifty-three closures of registered factories but sixty new registrations. With the outbreak of the Sino-Japanese War in 1937, there began a new period of expansion as Chinese firms, moving away from Japanese occupation, set up factories in the safety of Hong Kong. Steel-rolling, the manufacture of enamelware, needle-making and other metal industries were established in 1937 and 1938. At the same time, exports to Southeast Asian countries were increased as Japan's industries turned increasingly to meet its own military needs, and China's industrial goods were withdrawn from competition in the market. The outbreak of the Second World War in Europe provided a further stimulus to the manufacture of war necessities such as gas masks, metal helmets, spades and entrenching tools, water bottles, field telephones, and transmitting and receiving sets. Other industries, hitherto unknown to the Colony, started to manufacture bicycles, tabloid medicine, nails, tooth-brushes and buttons. Many Shanghai workers were brought into the Colony for these trades, especially for the printing industry. Many new factory-type premises were erected and a substantial demand existed for skilled and unskilled labour. In 1938, the number of factory workers was estimated at 55,000 which included only those in registered factories. This number had risen to about 90,000 in 1941.[35]

Till the end of the period under consideration, the Government had been content to provide security and sound administration, and to adopt a *laissez-faire* attitude towards industry, as it did towards trade. There was no legislation providing for the establishment of conciliatory machinery for the settlement of labour disputes, nor was there factory legislation controlling compensation for accidents or provision for sickness and old age. There was no control to regularize the quality of produce. The majority of the factories in the older industries were little more than workshops, using out-dated machinery. The shortage of capital and technical know-how prevented modernization.

Before the Pacific War, Hong Kong was still primarily a trading centre and only 10% of the total value of its exports was of locally-manufactured goods. The future of industry was not clear as many of the war-time developments were obviously temporary. Even in 1938, in the early days of Imperial Preference, the voluntary limitation of the export of rubber footwear was demanded by British manufacturers. Imports into Great Britain were restricted after the outbreak of war in Europe. Qualifications for Preference in other Commonwealth countries were highly variable. Until world conditions became more settled with the conclusion of the War, the industrial community in the Colony was able to do no more than its best in a difficult situation.

The Sino-Japanese War, begun in 1937, radically changed trading conditions for Hong Kong. Within the first six months of the Sino-Japanese War, the major sea routes connecting China and the outside world were cut off at Shanghai, Tientsin and Tsingtao. Canton and Hong Kong remained the only outlets for seaborne trade. Hong Kong's share in the trade of free unoccupied China rapidly increased while, in October 1938, China's coastal trade came to a virtual standstill when the Chinese Government ordered the complete prohibition of imports from Japan or from areas controlled by Japan (Table 12). This prohibition was withdrawn in June 1939 because of the urgency of obtaining certain

TABLE 12. PERCENTAGE OF CHINA'S FOREIGN TRADE
PASSING THROUGH HONG KONG, 1937–41

Year	Imports			Exports		
	All China	Occupied China	Free China	All China	Occupied China	Free China
1937	2·0			19·4		
1938	2·8	1·8	4·7	31·9	11·0	67·3
1939	2·6	1·4	13·8	21·6	14·8	51·7
1940	7·2	2·2	40·2	18·6	13·3	55·8
1941	14·5	1·8	58·3	25·5	17·6	78·9

SOURCE: Cheng Yu-Kwei, *Foreign trade*, 1956, p. 134, 135.

essential commodities. Hence quantities of cotton manufactures, cotton yarn, paper, chemicals, pharmaceutical preparations, sugar and other articles, manufactured either in the Japanese homeland or in occupied China, were shipped to Hong Kong for re-export to free China after relabelling and repacking. Under Japanese occupation, China's seaports were still open to shipping from Hong Kong and other western countries and China's coastal trade revived. Goods originating outside Japan and China were also repacked in Hong Kong to suit the rugged highway transport in free China after the Canton-Hankow railway was lost in 1938. Hong Kong thus enjoyed a period of brisk trading activity by virtue of its position in a divided China. Alternative routes were promptly opened by Hong Kong merchants as one Chinese port on the South China coast after another fell into Japanese hands. This trading activity continued up to the end of 1941 when Hong Kong itself was overrun.

CHAPTER FOUR

DESTRUCTION AND REHABILITATION, 1941-6

IN 1941, the year in which Hong Kong completed its first century of existence as a British Colony, this city of refuge became the scene of war and destruction. The rapid change in the physical, economic and political conditions in the Colony, brought about by the Japanese invasion in December 1941, was matched only by its speedy recovery under the British Military Administration, after liberation in August 1946. Considering the damage inflicted on the port by warfare, looting, and neglect by the Japanese for the three years and eight months of their occupation, it was a remarkable achievement of the re-occupation personnel, both government and civilian, that the normal functioning of the port was restored within a year. Civil government was re-instituted on 1 May 1946, by which time the port had been reopened to trade for nearly six months and was well on the way to another trade boom.

Although no precise date can be given for the restoration of the prosperity of the port, for this was a continuous and evolutionary process, the handing over of the government from military to civil administration can be taken as marking the conclusion of the period of rehabilitation. The capitulation of the Japanese on 14 August 1945 did not mark the end of the series of changes in the port that began with the outbreak of the Pacific War. The post-war rehabilitation is part of a phase in its history which is distinct from the normal course of its development. This chapter covers the period in which the port was under the military control of the Japanese and of the British, although the changes which took place under these two administrations are hardly comparable.

The strategic value of the Colony, which played a vital part in its foundation, was put to the test after only a hundred years of peaceful existence. The role of Hong Kong in the British Empire was that of a fortress and a trading post. It was the headquarters of the British China Squadron, an air base, and a second-class naval base.[1] The opinion that Hong Kong was practically invulnerable from the sea was commonly held while British naval supremacy was unchallenged in the Far East, but with the emergence of Japan in the early twentieth century as the third strongest naval power, the strategic value of the Colony was, at best, doubtful. Its position so close to Japanese naval and air bases in

Formosa and so remote from the nearest source of British reinforcement made it unsuitable as a naval base. This was the conclusion reached by the Committee of Imperial Defence in 1921.[2] By the Washington Treaties of 1922, Hong Kong was demilitarized and Singapore took over its position as a British fortress in the Far East. Preparations for war were resumed only after 1936 when Japan denounced the Washington Treaties. With Japanese occupation of areas around the Colony after October 1938, it was plain that it would be impossible to hold out against an enemy advance on the landward side. The sole reason for its defence was to deny the harbour to the Japanese. In the event of war, Hong Kong was to be regarded as an outpost to be held for as long as possible. With the limited force then available, the plan of defence was to withdraw to the Island, after the forward troops of the invaders had been slowed down, to allow time to clear the harbour and to destroy installations on the mainland.[3] As the Japanese attack became imminent on the morning of 8 December 1941, the first wave of destruction was set off by the defenders of the port who, in the course of four days, carried out the widespread demolition of plant and utilities that might be of use to the invaders. Installations and public utilities suffered heavy damage from military operations, houses, and shops, offices and godowns were subject to large-scale looting while the city was not subject to either British or Japanese control.

It is undoubtedly true that the material wealth of the city suffered more from looting than from military operations. Looting continued for nearly four years until the British Military Administration was set up in August 1945. The Japanese did the greatest share of the looting since they were able to do it systematically and over the longest period. The removal of equipment, machinery and stores from the Colony followed immediately upon its fall. One unofficial estimate reported that in the Kowloon godowns and docks alone, the Japanese seized no fewer than 2,500,000 tons of freight, and that Japanese vessels carried between 300,000 and 350,000 tons of seized materials to Japan each month.[4]

Damage caused by military operations did not cease with the surrender of the Colony. During the period of Japanese occupation, the Colony was subjected to frequent bombing raids that continued until the end of the Pacific War. The dockyard areas, used by the Japanese for the movement of supplies and for repairs, were the targets for destruction. A total of 140 bomb hits were recorded on the Kowloon premises of the Hong Kong and Whampoa Dock. The adjoining area of Hung Hom, where most of the dockyard workers lived, was razed. At the Taikoo Dockyard, in addition to the bombing of buildings and equipment, ships were sunk in the graving-dock and by the side of the surrounding seawalls. Wharves and shipbuilding berths were wrecked both above and below water. Launches and other light craft were also sunk while loading or discharging at the wharves, or in midstream. By the end of the Japanese occupation, the wrecks of eleven ships and seventy-two small craft choked the harbour.

The uncontended liberation of Hong Kong by British forces prevented further destruction, and yet, in the sixteen-day period between the Japanese capitulation, on 14 August, and the arrival of units of the British Pacific Fleet, on 30 August, looting again brought devastation to many unoccupied buildings and properties.

The Japanese inherited Hong Kong's population problems when they took over the control of the Colony from the British. The most urgent of these problems, the supply of food and accommodation, was aggravated by war-time destruction and by the cutting of the normal lines of supply. The Japanese remedy was to reduce demand by a systematic expulsion of almost a million people from the Colony. According to official statements published on 4 February 1942, in the *Hong Kong News,* 250,000 persons had left. This means an average reduction of 10,000 persons or more a day. In order to facilitate the repatriation, steamer traffic to Canton was reopened in January 1942, but mainly for passengers. A few days later the Hong Kong to Macao steamer traffic was resumed and, early in February, routes by sea were opened to Swatow, Chiu Chow, Kongmoon and Kwangchow Wan.

Figures published in the early summer of 1942 gave the total population as 1,074,176 while a broadcast from Tokyo, on 20 January 1943, gave the population of Hong Kong at the end of 1942 as 983,512. A further 150,000 to 200,000 probably left in the period 1943–5, while many others perished within Hong Kong. Towards the end of the Japanese occupation only about 500,000 people remained. According to the census taken by Air-Raid Wardens, just before the War, the population of the Colony was 1,640,000 which means that two-thirds of the people were removed as a result of the War. However, the Japanese administration was unable to provide adequate subsistence, even for this comparatively small population.

With the help of the Rehabilitation Committee composed of members of the Chinese Chamber of Commerce, the Japanese put tremendous efforts into the repair and resumption of essential services for the

convenience of the administration. Communications were among the
first to operate again. In addition to the opening of river and coastal
steamer services, the Canton-Kowloon railway was repaired and reopened
to local traffic in March 1942, and to through traffic to Canton in
December 1943. Cross-harbour ferries, scuttled in the battle, were
salvaged and put into service on reduced schedules, but public transport
on the roads was almost non-existent because most vehicles had been
shipped out of the Colony.

As far as the development of the port is concerned, the only improvement made under the Japanese occupation was the extension of the
Kai Tak airfield at the head of Kowloon Bay. Almost immediately after
the fall of Hong Kong, the Japanese repaired the airfield and used it for
military operations. The original airfield, dating from the late 1920s,
still consisted of a grass field without runways when it fell into Japanese
hands. The Japanese plan to enlarge it was first announced on 6 June
1942. The extension (Fig. 14) incorporated land to the north and west,

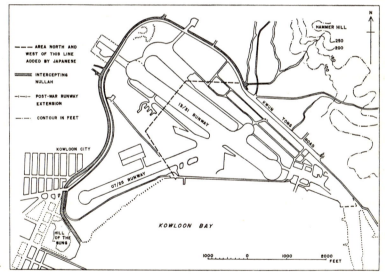

Figure 14. Kai Tak airport extension, 1941–6.

the latter involving the demolition of a large area of Kowloon City, part
of the Hill of Sung, and the reclamation of about thirty acres. Some
forty factories, twenty small villages and numerous individual buildings
were removed. Using mainly prisoner-of-war labour, the new airfield

with two runways was completed in the summer of 1943. Owing to the lack of material, the runways were not well constructed and their use by heavy aircraft after the war soon made them unserviceable. After slight modifications and repair, however, these runways served the aviation purposes of the Colony for over twelve years after the end of the Pacific War. The present new runway was not ready for service until 1958.

Following the occupation by the Japanese, the external trade of the Colony was cut off. There was no commercial shipping in the harbour. The opening of the coastal routes had little significance except for repatriation purposes. Internal trade was negligible since the Japanese military seized all stocks in the godowns and sealed or dismantled factories after depriving them of their labour force. No resumption of commercial or industrial activities could take place without Japanese consent. Any application for permission to reopen business had to give the most detailed information, including a surface plan of the place of business and a construction plan. Owners of stock in godowns were to apply for the release of goods, which often led to extortion and 'squeeze'. In many cases, the owners had to give up their claims and leave the Colony as best they could. In the field of industry, a Chinese Manufacturers' Union was formed to seek official assistance for the resumption of operations, but the same procedure of bribery and extortion prevailed. The Japanese used outright confiscation to enforce their participation in the supervision and ownership of Hong Kong firms and factories, which allowed them to reorganize commercial and industrial activities to suit their own needs.

The food-processing industries were among the first to resume operation. The cement works at Hung Hom, which supplied most local construction material, resumed production in January 1943. The arrival in the later part of 1942 of raw materials from Japanese-occupied Southeast Asia and China led to more industrial activity. By June 1943, the military authorities reported 800 'industrial plants' operating full time, though many of these plants were little more than family workshops where production depended entirely on manual labour. Industries in which machinery was used to some extent included sugar-refining, silk-spinning, canning, and the manufacture of rubber goods (eg. shoes, tyres, tubes, hoses and boots), electric machines and ropes. It was stated that 70% of all products was exported, local markets absorbing the balance. A series of trading agreements were concluded with other Japanese-occupied territories for the exchange of essential materials. Hong Kong exported cotton goods, rubber articles, cloth, seafood, matches and Chinese medicine to Hainan, and imported in return salt, raw rubber, crude sugar and other agricultural produce. Electrical appliances, automobile parts, engineering materials, textiles, sugar, rubber products, salt and dried fish were sent to Canton in exchange for rice, silk, native tobacco, meat, fresh and dried vegetables, eggs and fruit. It will be noticed that this trade was essentially an exchange of manufactured articles for raw materials and foodstuffs, generated by the need for survival rather than by the desire for economic development. Even this trade diminished gradually, owing to the shortage of Japanese shipping as the war turned more and more in favour of the Allies. Hong Kong's share in the imports of occupied China was only 2% (US$2,485,000) in 1942, dwindling to 0·5% (US$70,000) for the period January to August 1945.[5] Of the exports of occupied China 1·5% (US$666,000) went to Hong Kong in 1942; the corresponding figure for 1945 was 0·7% (US$50,700).

TABLE 13.   HONG KONG IMPORTS INTO FREE CHINA, 1942–5

Year	Total value of imports into Free China (US$)	Imports passing through Hong Kong	
		Value (US$)	Percentage
1942	41,504,000	4,440,900	10·7
1943	48,906,000	7,091,300	14·5
1944	17,327,000	2,737,600	15·8
1945*	7,028,000	934,700	13·3

SOURCE: Cheng, Yu-Kwei, *Foreign Trade and Industrial Development of China*, 1956, Table 55.
* Jan. to Aug.

Between Free China and Hong Kong, trade was continuous despite Japanese orders in January 1942 prohibiting the movement of goods to or from enemy territories. The import of industrial and consumer essentials, irrespective of their origin, was encouraged by Free China, which had been cut off from its western allies by both sea and land after the spring of 1942. Private traders managed to filter these goods through in small but numerous lots, sometimes by very intricate routes. Records were necessarily confusing and do not provide a full account of the trade. The Customs Office of Free China did not keep track of exports, which were considered secret. As the above table shows, the percentage of imports coming from Hong Kong increased after 1942, when Free China depended heavily on goods of Japanese and German origin. In terms of actual values, trade sharply declined after 1943 as Free China's resources were exhausted.

No just appraisal of the far-reaching consequences of the War for Hong Kong is possible without looking into the political situation. Even before war was declared between Great Britain and Japan, much attention had been drawn to the political position of Hong Kong, in the event of a Chinese victory.[6] The question arose largely from the unalterable fact that the Colony was not only geographically a part of China, but also, as the accumulated experience of a century indicated, it was, economically and socially, a part of China. The status of the Colony was impermanent in the light of the growth of national self-consciousness in China, accelerated by the Japanese invasion. On the other hand, its continued separate existence as a free port had great economic advantages for all. In relation to China, the importance of Hong Kong lay not only in its trade contacts, but also in the educational influence of its modern economic activities on a country of economic backwardness and political unrest.

The entry of China into the Second World War as a full partner of the Allies strengthened the hand of its Government in pressing for the abolition of such treaties as they considered unequal. In an attempt to foster the morale of the Chinese in the darkest days of the War, a treaty was signed in Chungking on 11 January 1943, by which Great Britain and all British Colonies and Dependencies agreed to relinquish all extra-territorial rights in China. Under an exchange of notes accompanying the Treaty, Great Britain also relinquished her rights of coasting trade and inland navigation in Chinese waters. Although there had been some cause for uneasiness about the possible full implementation of the principles contained in these Treaties, provision had been made for further negotiations to determine the comprehensive instruments of trade and navigation. In view of China's need for foreign technical and financial assistance in post-war reconstruction, an illiberal and restrictive attitude would not serve her true interests, yet it was by no means certain that British rule in Hong Kong would be restored. Further complications over the political status of the Colony arose because Hong Kong fell within the area of military operations controlled by Chinese forces and because the Colony was not recovered as the result of a military operation.

It is not the intention of the present study to trace the details of conferences and delicate operations that led to the resumption of British

1. Detail of a perspective drawing (1842) of Hong Kong looking west from above Causeway Bay. One year after its cession to the British Government the island was only scantily settled. *From the Collection of the City Museum and Art Gallery, Urban Council, Hong Kong.*

2. By 1860, as can be seen in this view of Victoria Harbour looking west, there had been substantial building of commercial and residential accommodation. *From the Collection of the City Museum and Art Gallery, Urban Council, Hong Kong.*

3. The centre of European mercantile activity was early established at the Victoria waterfront (photo 1870). *From the Collection of the City Museum and Art Gallery, Urban Council, Hong Kong.*

4.   The long-established practice of overside delivery of cargo from ship to lighters is still common in Hong Kong despite the trend towards containerization. *Photo : Hong Kong Government Information Services.*

5.   At the Western Praya junks and lighters bring ashore produce direct from China and cargo from ships moored in the harbour. This section of the waterfront is often acutely congested. *Photo : Hong Kong Government Information Services.*

n major industries,[11] including the Taikoo Dockyard, the [
al Dockyard, the Hong Kong and Whampoa Docks, the [
pany, the electric light and power companies, and the two [
ur ferry companies. The high wage claims, although justifie[
post-war level of price indices (shown in Table 14), tended to r[
ess in the reorganization of production.

TABLE 14. WHOLESALE PRICE INDICES, 1939–46 (1938 = 100)

	1939	1940	1941*	1
odstuffs	96·8	124·6	155·4	70
xtiles	91·2	124·8	138·3	76
tals and minerals	100·0	142·8	160·2	28
cellaneous	100·4	138·4	168·9	60

E: Hong Kong Government, *Annual Report*, 1946.
t six months of the year.

der the British Military Administration, the Department
lies and Industry functioned as the principal trading organizat
sive trade control measures were introduced to guarantee
es in short supply should reach local markets and be retained th
Department dispatched special missions to all neighbou
ries to obtain essential supplies: Shanghai and Hongay for c
ngchow Wan for vegetable oil; Borneo for firewood; Australi
ng material and household goods; and Malaya for rubber.
al months, Hong Kong was unable to obtain from outside
y of cotton yarn for the restarting of its textile industry,
vised measures were adopted to make full use of local stock. S
yarn as the Japanese had left was requisitioned and turned o
tain weaving factories for conversion into canvas so that
r-shoe industry could reopen to supply local demand. The wo
ge of textiles, probably more acute than the world food shorta
y affected the Colony's economy, since it left knitting, weav
arment-making factories idle for lack of material, and restric
olony's entrepôt trade. The early resumption of normal trade
ly urged by the business community in order to improve sup
ions and to profit from Hong Kong's apparent advantage o
ports in China. Yielding to public demand, the British Milita
istration declared the port opened to trading on 23 Novemb
two months earlier than was originally planned. Trade control

6. A liner moored at the Ocean Terminal, which can accommodate up to four ocean-going liners. The terminal was opened in 1966. *Photo : Hong Kong Government Information Services.*

7. Frequent cross-harbour ferry services, passenger and vehicular, add to the congestion of a busy port. *Photo : Hong Kong Government Information Services.*

8. Part of the Hong Kong and Kowloon Wharf and Godown Company's container complex at Tsim Sha Tsui. *Photo: Hong Kong Government Information Services.*

9. Reclamation has been a recurrent feature in the development of Hong Kong. This extensive project was necessary for the construction of the container terminal at Kwai Chung. *Photo: Hong Kong Government Information Services.*

authority in Hong Kong. It is sufficient to note
did not pass unchallenged.[7] Important to the dev
however, were the obstacles to the work of reh
national feelings among the Chinese residents in the
incidents and riots in the period immediately
prevented from spreading only by the judicious co
tration, with the support of the law-abiding eleme
whose only desire was the return to normal funct
peace and security. For safety, it was found ne
Military Administration from April to May 1946.
the recovery of Hong Kong compared favourably
'scarcely a shop was open and the Military Adn
till the middle of 1946.'[8]

As soon as British rule was re-established in H
an influx of people from South China. The m
pre-war immigrants who had left during the V
control, imposed since 1940, was nominally in for
a half months after re-occupation, but no m
restriction existed and it was regarded with in
the Chinese authorities. As a gesture designed
relations with China, this restriction was lifted.
500,000 at the time the Japanese left, the Color
about one million by the end of 1945, and subse
estimated rate of 100,000 per month.[9] A serious s
tion resulted, and overcrowding, a social proble
Colony and eliminated by crude methods dur
along with the peace. While the population f
levels in less than a year, little was done to rest
The Building Reconstruction Advisory Commi
out a survey of housing conditions and to n
rehabilitation, recorded a total of 20,506 b
displacing 160,837 persons.[10] This figure took n
to buildings belonging to the Services, which p
problem, as they had to accommodate an un
H.M. Forces.

Lack of material and labour and the Rents Or
property owners from increasing rent although
very considerably, slowed reconstruction worl
adjustment, the high cost of living with its
demands gave rise to a series of short strikes in

still exercised through a system of import and export licensing. Towards the middle of 1946, it was found possible to dispense with the export control on all commodities except those under world allocation or in short supply in Hong Kong. The licensing of imports was maintained throughout the period.

Owing to the concentrated effort of the post-war import drive, the port facilities of Hong Kong were among the first to be rehabilitated, for on their efficient functioning depended not only the supplies of the Colony but also the transfer of much-needed relief material to South China. In anticipation of the organization work required to bring the port back into operation after the return of British rule, a number of internees in prisoner camps had prepared a complete scheme for taking over port administration. On the liberation of the Colony a central organization, known as the Port Executive Committee, was set up. At the same time a Port Working Committee was established to carry out the policy laid down by the Port Executive Committee. Another organization, the Far Eastern Shipping Agencies, was established to deal with the handling of ocean and coastal shipping running on government account and the allocation of shipping and facilities.

Apart from damage by military operations, the port facilities suffered severely from neglect and lack of maintenance. Of the five wharves of the Hong Kong and Kowloon Wharf and Godown Company, one was damaged beyond repair and the remainder needed major repair. Only half of Holt's wharves were serviceable. Not a single steam or electric crane was in working order, and of the 2,000 craft used as lighters or short distance cargo boats before the War, only 500 could be mustered. Only two of the forty-eight commercial moorings survived, and the harbour was littered with wrecks. While repairs and salvage had to be done with a minimum of constructional material and equipment, the chief difficulty in the operation of the port was the acute shortage of godown space. A quarter of the public warehouse space (95,000 tons out of 400,000) had been destroyed during the War. Those warehouses still standing were stocked with Japanese equipment. The Godown Committee did much useful work in finding alternative accommodation. The improved railway service also helped to relieve congestion of goods in the port. The return of the Chinese people to Hong Kong was concurrent with the gradual increase in shipping using the port. The increasing supply of unskilled labour improved the rate of loading and discharge of ships. By the end of the Military Administration, the normal operation of the port had been restored.

Abnormal conditions of demand produced a trade boom soon after the War. The total value of foreign trade was in excess of the pre-war level by March 1946. On account of higher prices, it would be necessary to reduce this total by two-thirds before comparing it with the 1939 volume of trade. However, no accurate measure of the volume of goods passing through the port is possible since these figures include neither transhipment cargoes nor supplies brought in by the Military Administration and UNRRA.[12] With shipping space in high demand and the Western countries slowly recovering from the exhaustion of the War, Hong Kong could depend only on countries bordering the Pacific Ocean for the bulk of its trade. After China, the United States took the largest share. India was the only country outside the Pacific area with which the Colony had significant trading connections. Commercial relationships were building up with the Philippines, Malaya and French Indo-China, while trade with Japan was re-opened, but only on a government-to-government basis. In the first few months of the resumption of normal trading, foodstuffs formed the major imports; as general rehabilitation got under way, the demand shifted to textiles and capital goods.

Industry did not recover quite as quickly as trade, being handicapped by the shortage of material and the loss of machinery. On the other hand, markets were easy to find because Chinese and Japanese products were temporarily removed from competition. Industries that depended on the supply of raw material from China were the first to resume production at or near pre-war levels. Among such industries were tobacco, matches and paint-making. Restored on a small scale were the manufacture of soap, rattanware, rubber and canvas shoes, nails and leather goods, boat-building, and flour and rice milling. At the end of 1946, the general level of industrial activity was estimated to be at 20% of pre-war capacity.

Although the prosperity of the port still lagged far behind pre-war standards, there was no doubt that the recovery of Hong Kong had been rapid and substantial. By May 1946, foreign correspondents were reporting that 'nowhere in Southeast Asia do you find so many encouraging signs as in Hong Kong.'[13] 'Generally speaking, Hong Kong seems to have recovered to a far greater extent than any other trading centre east of India.'[14] The major factors leading to this recovery were: the speedy establishment of law and order and a stable currency, providing security for commercial transactions; the insatiable demand for food and consumer goods of the Far Eastern markets, starved for three and a half years; the fact that the port facilities had not been entirely disabled by the War; the early return of Chinese people with their enterprise and resilience to develop all sources of supplies; and, finally, the preservation of Hong Kong's traditional status as a free port, with minimum restrictions on trade and finance.

In relation to the China trade, Hong Kong has assumed greater importance in the post-war period. Now that there are no longer any foreign concessions left in other ports or towns in the interior, Hong Kong has come to be the centre of foreign population and economic interests. There was hardly a British firm in Shanghai which did not eventually transfer its principal office to Hong Kong. Many Chinese firms with foreign trade connections have followed. Post-war conditions in China have not, however, favoured the development of foreign trade. Yielding to nationalist sentiment, the Chinese Government excluded foreign-flag vessels from the inland waterways and coastal trade. The heavy excess of imports and an inflated currency weakened the Chinese market while, immediately following the Japanese surrender in the autumn of 1945, civil war broke out in the north-east. Hong Kong merchants were already apprehensive lest the extreme difficulties with which exports to China had to contend might compel them to abandon the market altogether.

RECONSTRUCTION AND INDUSTRIALIZATION, 1946-50

THE entrepôt function of Hong Kong was resumed as soon as the port was reopened to commercial trading in November 1945, although the conditions under which trading was conducted could hardly be described as normal. Commodities and shipping, the two essentials on which port activities depended, were both lacking in the world market. Foodstuffs and textiles, the leading items in the entrepôt trade of Hong Kong before the War, were placed under international allocation. Government control of essential supplies was maintained until 1948, although it was administered as liberally as international obligations of commodity allocation would allow. The number of controlled items diminished gradually with the return to normality of world production.

The important part played by economic liberalism in the development of Hong Kong cannot be overstressed. This has been recognized by various students of its evolution.[1] It is worth inquiring, however, how far the faithful pursuance of a *laissez-faire* policy has been the result of far-sighted planning and how far the result of immediate economic necessity. In the period immediately after the War, the combined effect of rehabilitation in Southeast Asia and of the shortage of raw materials, machines and foodstuffs was to urge the resumption of trade. This amounted to the re-distribution and allocation of stocks concentrated in certain areas by the Japanese, before manufacturing and primary production could be reorganized. The established services and commercial links of Hong Kong were in immediate demand from importers in China and other Southeast Asian countries. In response to this demand there was a mushroom growth of businesses in the Colony in 1946.[2] The return to an entrepôt economy meant the return to dependence on economic and political conditions outside Hong Kong's control. Adaptability and resilience were particularly needed in coping with the unstable situation of commercial regulations in China. No rigid control or adherence to long-term plans was practicable.

Trade with China was prosperous in the first three quarters of the year 1946, for the Chinese Government put tremendous efforts into stimulating exports, in an attempt to lighten the excess of imports. High

6.   A liner moored at the Ocean Terminal, which can accommodate up to four ocean-going liners. The terminal was opened in 1966. *Photo : Hong Kong Government Information Services.*

7.   Frequent cross-harbour ferry services, passenger and vehicular, add to the congestion of a busy port. *Photo : Hong Kong Government Information Services.*

8. Part of the Hong Kong and Kowloon Wharf and Godown Company's container complex at Tsim Sha Tsui. *Photo : Hong Kong Government Information Services.*

9. Reclamation has been a recurrent feature in the development of Hong Kong. This extensive project was necessary for the construction of the container terminal at Kwai Chung. *Photo : Hong Kong Government Information Services.*

authority in Hong Kong. It is sufficient to note that this resumption did not pass unchallenged.[7] Important to the development of the port, however, were the obstacles to the work of rehabilitation created by national feelings among the Chinese residents in the Colony. Anti-foreign incidents and riots in the period immediately after the War were prevented from spreading only by the judicious conduct of the Administration, with the support of the law-abiding elements of the community, whose only desire was the return to normal functioning of the port, in peace and security. For safety, it was found necessary to extend the Military Administration from April to May 1946. Even with this delay, the recovery of Hong Kong compared favourably with Singapore, where 'scarcely a shop was open and the Military Administration carried on till the middle of 1946.'[8]

As soon as British rule was re-established in Hong Kong, there began an influx of people from South China. The majority of these were pre-war immigrants who had left during the War. The immigration control, imposed since 1940, was nominally in force for the first two and a half months after re-occupation, but no means of enforcing this restriction existed and it was regarded with increasing resentment by the Chinese authorities. As a gesture designed to re-establish friendly relations with China, this restriction was lifted. From a figure of about 500,000 at the time the Japanese left, the Colony's population grew to about one million by the end of 1945, and subsequently increased at an estimated rate of 100,000 per month.[9] A serious shortage of accommodation resulted, and overcrowding, a social problem characteristic of the Colony and eliminated by crude methods during the War, returned along with the peace. While the population figure regained pre-war levels in less than a year, little was done to restore damaged buildings. The Building Reconstruction Advisory Committee, appointed to carry out a survey of housing conditions and to recommend policies for rehabilitation, recorded a total of 20,506 building units damaged, displacing 160,837 persons.[10] This figure took no account of the damage to buildings belonging to the Services, which probably posed a greater problem, as they had to accommodate an unusually large number of H.M. Forces.

Lack of material and labour and the Rents Ordinance, which prevented property owners from increasing rent although building costs had risen very considerably, slowed reconstruction work. During this period of adjustment, the high cost of living with its consequent high wage demands gave rise to a series of short strikes in the public utilities as well as in major industries,[11] including the Taikoo Dockyard, the Royal Naval Dockyard, the Hong Kong and Whampoa Docks, the Gas Company, the electric light and power companies, and the two cross-habour ferry companies. The high wage claims, although justified by the post-war level of price indices (shown in Table 14), tended to retard progress in the reorganization of production.

TABLE 14. WHOLESALE PRICE INDICES, 1939–46 (1938 = 100)

	1939	*1940*	*1941**	*1946*
Foodstuffs	96·8	124·6	155·4	704·8
Textiles	91·2	124·8	138·3	769·1
Metals and minerals	100·0	142·8	160·2	287·3
Miscellaneous	100·4	138·4	168·9	604·5

SOURCE: Hong Kong Government, *Annual Report,* 1946.
* First six months of the year.

Under the British Military Administration, the Department of Supplies and Industry functioned as the principal trading organization. Extensive trade control measures were introduced to guarantee that articles in short supply should reach local markets and be retained there. The Department dispatched special missions to all neighbouring countries to obtain essential supplies: Shanghai and Hongay for coal; Kwangchow Wan for vegetable oil; Borneo for firewood; Australia for building material and household goods; and Malaya for rubber. For several months, Hong Kong was unable to obtain from outside any supply of cotton yarn for the restarting of its textile industry, and improvised measures were adopted to make full use of local stock. Such cotton yarn as the Japanese had left was requisitioned and turned over to certain weaving factories for conversion into canvas so that the rubber-shoe industry could reopen to supply local demand. The world shortage of textiles, probably more acute than the world food shortage, gravely affected the Colony's economy, since it left knitting, weaving and garment-making factories idle for lack of material, and restricted the Colony's entrepôt trade. The early resumption of normal trade was strongly urged by the business community in order to improve supply conditions and to profit from Hong Kong's apparent advantage over rival ports in China. Yielding to public demand, the British Military Administration declared the port opened to trading on 23 November 1945, two months earlier than was originally planned. Trade control was still exercised through a system of import and export licensing. Towards the middle of 1946, it was found possible to dispense with the export control on all commodities except those under world allocation or in short supply in Hong Kong. The licensing of imports was maintained throughout the period.

Owing to the concentrated effort of the post-war import drive, the port facilities of Hong Kong were among the first to be rehabilitated, for on their efficient functioning depended not only the supplies of the Colony but also the transfer of much-needed relief material to South China. In anticipation of the organization work required to bring the port back into operation after the return of British rule, a number of internees in prisoner camps had prepared a complete scheme for taking over port administration. On the liberation of the Colony a central organization, known as the Port Executive Committee, was set up. At the same time a Port Working Committee was established to carry out the policy laid down by the Port Executive Committee. Another organization, the Far Eastern Shipping Agencies, was established to deal with the handling of ocean and coastal shipping running on government account and the allocation of shipping and facilities.

Apart from damage by military operations, the port facilities suffered severely from neglect and lack of maintenance. Of the five wharves of the Hong Kong and Kowloon Wharf and Godown Company, one was damaged beyond repair and the remainder needed major repair. Only half of Holt's wharves were serviceable. Not a single steam or electric crane was in working order, and of the 2,000 craft used as lighters or short distance cargo boats before the War, only 500 could be mustered. Only two of the forty-eight commercial moorings survived, and the harbour was littered with wrecks. While repairs and salvage had to be done with a minimum of constructional material and equipment, the chief difficulty in the operation of the port was the acute shortage of godown space. A quarter of the public warehouse space (95,000 tons out of 400,000) had been destroyed during the War. Those warehouses still standing were stocked with Japanese equipment. The Godown Committee did much useful work in finding alternative accommodation. The improved railway service also helped to relieve congestion of goods in the port. The return of the Chinese people to Hong Kong was concurrent with the gradual increase in shipping using the port. The increasing supply of unskilled labour improved the rate of loading and discharge of ships. By the end of the Military Administration, the normal operation of the port had been restored.

Abnormal conditions of demand produced a trade boom soon after the War. The total value of foreign trade was in excess of the pre-war level by March 1946. On account of higher prices, it would be necessary to reduce this total by two-thirds before comparing it with the 1939 volume of trade. However, no accurate measure of the volume of goods passing through the port is possible since these figures include neither transhipment cargoes nor supplies brought in by the Military Administration and UNRRA.[12] With shipping space in high demand and the Western countries slowly recovering from the exhaustion of the War, Hong Kong could depend only on countries bordering the Pacific Ocean for the bulk of its trade. After China, the United States took the largest share. India was the only country outside the Pacific area with which the Colony had significant trading connections. Commercial relationships were building up with the Philippines, Malaya and French Indo-China, while trade with Japan was re-opened, but only on a government-to-government basis. In the first few months of the resumption of normal trading, foodstuffs formed the major imports; as general rehabilitation got under way, the demand shifted to textiles and capital goods.

Industry did not recover quite as quickly as trade, being handicapped by the shortage of material and the loss of machinery. On the other hand, markets were easy to find because Chinese and Japanese products were temporarily removed from competition. Industries that depended on the supply of raw material from China were the first to resume production at or near pre-war levels. Among such industries were tobacco, matches and paint-making. Restored on a small scale were the manufacture of soap, rattanware, rubber and canvas shoes, nails and leather goods, boat-building, and flour and rice milling. At the end of 1946, the general level of industrial activity was estimated to be at 20% of pre-war capacity.

Although the prosperity of the port still lagged far behind pre-war standards, there was no doubt that the recovery of Hong Kong had been rapid and substantial. By May 1946, foreign correspondents were reporting that 'nowhere in Southeast Asia do you find so many encouraging signs as in Hong Kong.'[13] 'Generally speaking, Hong Kong seems to have recovered to a far greater extent than any other trading centre east of India.'[14] The major factors leading to this recovery were: the speedy establishment of law and order and a stable currency, providing security for commercial transactions; the insatiable demand for food and consumer goods of the Far Eastern markets, starved for three and a half years; the fact that the port facilities had not been entirely disabled by the War; the early return of Chinese people with their enterprise and resilience to develop all sources of supplies; and, finally, the preservation of Hong Kong's traditional status as a free port, with minimum restrictions on trade and finance.

In relation to the China trade, Hong Kong has assumed greater importance in the post-war period. Now that there are no longer any foreign concessions left in other ports or towns in the interior, Hong Kong has come to be the centre of foreign population and economic interests. There was hardly a British firm in Shanghai which did not eventually transfer its principal office to Hong Kong. Many Chinese firms with foreign trade connections have followed. Post-war conditions in China have not, however, favoured the development of foreign trade. Yielding to nationalist sentiment, the Chinese Government excluded foreign-flag vessels from the inland waterways and coastal trade. The heavy excess of imports and an inflated currency weakened the Chinese market while, immediately following the Japanese surrender in the autumn of 1945, civil war broke out in the north-east. Hong Kong merchants were already apprehensive lest the extreme difficulties with which exports to China had to contend might compel them to abandon the market altogether.

RECONSTRUCTION AND
INDUSTRIALIZATION, 1946-50

THE entrepôt function of Hong Kong was resumed as soon as the port was reopened to commercial trading in November 1945, although the conditions under which trading was conducted could hardly be described as normal. Commodities and shipping, the two essentials on which port activities depended, were both lacking in the world market. Foodstuffs and textiles, the leading items in the entrepôt trade of Hong Kong before the War, were placed under international allocation. Government control of essential supplies was maintained until 1948, although it was administered as liberally as international obligations of commodity allocation would allow. The number of controlled items diminished gradually with the return to normality of world production.

The important part played by economic liberalism in the development of Hong Kong cannot be overstressed. This has been recognized by various students of its evolution.[1] It is worth inquiring, however, how far the faithful pursuance of a *laissez-faire* policy has been the result of far-sighted planning and how far the result of immediate economic necessity. In the period immediately after the War, the combined effect of rehabilitation in Southeast Asia and of the shortage of raw materials, machines and foodstuffs was to urge the resumption of trade. This amounted to the re-distribution and allocation of stocks concentrated in certain areas by the Japanese, before manufacturing and primary production could be reorganized. The established services and commercial links of Hong Kong were in immediate demand from importers in China and other Southeast Asian countries. In response to this demand there was a mushroom growth of businesses in the Colony in 1946.[2] The return to an entrepôt economy meant the return to dependence on economic and political conditions outside Hong Kong's control. Adaptability and resilience were particularly needed in coping with the unstable situation of commercial regulations in China. No rigid control or adherence to long-term plans was practicable.

Trade with China was prosperous in the first three quarters of the year 1946, for the Chinese Government put tremendous efforts into stimulating exports, in an attempt to lighten the excess of imports. High profits were reaped by Hong Kong merchants. Conditions changed, however, during the later months of the year. The persistently unfavourable trade balance for China, amounting to US$412 millions in 1946, made it impossible for her to wait for the substantial revival of her exports. The official Chinese policy of preventing the employment of foreign shipping in inland waterways militated against economic recovery, since China's shipping was quite inadequate to cope with the demand for cargo space. The cost of handling goods at Chinese ports was prohibitive because of the absence of mechanical facilities. 'All cargo that can possibly be handled by coolies, or teams of coolies, are carried ashore; where this is impossible, the cargo is lowered into a lighter or sampan alongside and taken to some point where it can be man-handled ashore on rollers. This cumbersome procedure consumes a great deal of time and labour and is therefore very costly in wages.'[3] Stocks which the world required were piled up in collecting centres or were brought to ocean ports at enormous cost. China's post-war export drive thus failed and the Chinese Government had to reduce the volume of imports because of exchange difficulties. Their *Revised Temporary Foreign Trade Regulations* became effective from 18 November 1946, extending a licensing system to cover imports of all goods. Imports were divided into categories which were subject to different treatment. Essentials like industrial raw material and machinery were admitted with the least restriction while a wide variety of consumer goods was excluded altogether.

The trade boom that prevailed in Hong Kong in the period following the War was therefore arrested towards the end of 1946, but not before the pre-war pattern of entrepôt trade with China had been improved on. Table 15 compares the 1946 value of Hong Kong's trade with that of 1939, the last pre-war year for which figures are available. It has already been pointed out in the last chapter that increases in the value of trade should not be taken as a measure of growth.[4] The table provides, however, a clear picture of the direction of trade. The share of China in the trade of the Colony had grown from 28·6% to 36·5% (imports and exports), and it took 39·3% of Hong Kong exports in 1946 as compared with 16·9% in 1939. Other significant changes were the disappearance of Japan and Germany from the 1946 figures, and the rise in the shares of India and Malaya in the post-war period. The trend towards developing trade with Southeast Asian countries was beginning to show. Table

TABLE 15. HONG KONG IMPORTS AND EXPORTS BY COUNTRIES, 1939 AND 1946
(IN MILLIONS HK$)

Countries*	Imports from				Exports to			
	1939		1946		1939		1946	
	Value	%	Value	%	Value	%	Value	%
China	233·2	39·2	327·2	35·0	90·2	16·9	301·4	39·3
Macao	32·9	5·5	78·6	8·4	45·0	8·4	33·6	4·4
Kwangchow Wan	26·4	4·4	5·3	0·5	42·3	8·0	3·2	0·4
British Malaya	13·0	2·1	69·3	7·4	46·0	8·6	161·9	21·1
U.S.A.	51·9	8·7	119·6	12·8	76·9	14·4	83·7	10·9
French Indo-China	40·7	6·6	59·1	6·3	55·5	10·3	32·3	4·2
India	9·6	1·6	55·5	5·9	9·4	1·7	21·9	2·8
Siam	29·9	5·0	29·4	3·1	15·5	2·8	46·0	6·0
United Kingdom	39·7	6·5	43·9	4·6	22·4	4·2	16·6	2·1
Australia	7·1	1·2	42·6	4·5	3·9	0·7	4·2	0·5
Other British Empire	7·6	1·2	25·9	2·7	22·6	4·2	9·4	1·2
Philippines	2·6	0·4	16·0	1·7	11·4	2·1	18·0	2·3
Canada	4·8	0·8	11·2	1·2	2·6	0·5	0·8	0·1
Dutch East Indies	39·4	6·5	5·1	0·5	15·2	2·8	4·6	0·6
Japan	27·4	4·5	—	—	6·6	1·2	0·2	0·2
Germany	13·1	2·2	—	—	12·6	2·0	—	—
Other countries	24·9	4·2	46·8	5·0	55·3	10·3	27·8	3·6
Total	594·2	100	935·5	100	533·4	100	765·6	100

* Arranged in descending order by 1946 values of imports and exports, except for China, Macao and Kwangchow Wan which can be taken together as 'All China'.
SOURCE: Great Britain, Board of Trade, *Report of the United Kingdom Trade Mission to China, October to December, 1946*. London, 1948.

16 shows that, in 1946 as in 1939, the chief items of import were also the main exports, a pattern of trade which is typical of an entrepôt. It should be pointed out, however, that the high proportion of trade in piecegoods and textiles was a consequence of the Chinese Government's policy to export through Hong Kong a large share of its cotton products. This should be distinguished from the similarly important position occupied by locally-manufactured cotton textiles in the foreign trade of Hong Kong in subsequent years. Perhaps, however, the establishment of commercial links and the experience gained from handling the Chinese textile trade were not unrelated to the growth of the textile industries in the Colony in the late 1940s.

TABLE 16. HONG KONG IMPORTS AND EXPORTS BY MAIN CATEGORIES OF GOODS, 1939 AND 1946 (IN MILLIONS HK$)

Goods*	1939		1946	
	Imports	Exports	Imports	Exports
Foodstuffs and provisions	137·4	108·8	209·0	116·1
Oil and fat	89·4	75·0	114·0	142·9
Piecegoods and textiles	99·2	72·6	100·9	128·9
Chinese medicines	25·8	23·3	66·0	60·0
Metal	37·0	37·5	40·0	39·7
Paper and paperware	10·6	8·4	40·9	31·6
Chemicals and drugs	7·7	6·9	28·3	22·8
Nuts and seeds	9·9	6·5	22·1	11·9
Animals, live	14·2	0·5	32·1	—
Tobacco	9·6	9·7	25·3	6·2
Wearing apparel	4·4	28·6	10·5	18·7
Building material	7·7	3·1	20·9	3·3
Dyeing & tanning materials	8·1	8·8	11·6	8·3
Liquor, intoxicating	4·9	1·5	11·4	6·3
Vehicles	13·6	20·5	15·3	2·0
Hardware	4·7	4·4	4·9	8·5
Fuel	16·4	0.7	12·0	0.9
Paint	1·9	1·8	4·0	4·1
Machinery and engines	10·7	7·0	6·2	1·4
Manure	7·7	8·1	1·3	4·2
Mineral and ore	5·6	22·5	1·5	1·8
Railway material	0.1	0.1	0·01	0.02
Miscellaneous	67·4	77·3	155·1	146·0
Total	594·2	533·4	935·5	765·6

* Arranged in descending order by 1946 total values of imports and exports.
SOURCE: Great Britain, Board of Trade, 1947.

Trading conditions in China worsened after 1946 on account of the general disintegration of economic conditions, inflation, labour unrest and civil war. Severe restrictions on imports led to a widespread cancellation of orders for foreign goods. Cargoes on their way to Chinese ports were refused entry. The immediate consequences to Hong Kong were serious overstocking of commodities and congestion in warehouses as a result of the dumping of cargoes diverted from Shanghai and other Chinese ports; the failure of many merchant houses established since the war; and the elimination of the more speculative elements in trade. The internal commercial framework of Hong Kong quickly reverted to its pre-war pattern, in which trade was dominated by the older established and financially more secure merchant houses. Of far-reaching influence in the development of the port was the immigration of labour and capital, which began to build up at this time, sometimes in the form of whole manufacturing plants and firms along with their business connections. A strong urge grew among the merchant community for developing overseas markets, particularly in Commonwealth countries. The significance of industries in the Colony was growing, although they remained throughout the decade of secondary importance to the entrepôt trade.

The share taken by China in the trade of Hong Kong continued to diminish during the three years of civil war (1946–9). On the other hand, there was a sustained increase in the value of Hong Kong trade, by 62·8% in 1947 and 32·3% in 1948. This rate of growth is in large part attributable to the fact that the scarcity value of consumer goods during the early days of post-war rehabilitation was disappearing in 1947 and 1948.[5]

TABLE 17. THE POSITION OF CHINA IN THE TRADE OF HONG KONG, 1946–8

	1946	*1947*	*1948*
Total trade value, Hong Kong, (millions HK$)	1,699	2,766	3,660
Trade with China	628	641	711
China percentage	36·5%	23·2%	19·4%

SOURCE: Hong Kong, Imports and Exports Department, *Annual Report, 1946–8.*

Table 17 shows a slight increase in the actual value of trade with China, but this is far from comparable with the rate of increase for Hong Kong as a whole. Moreover, the increase in trade with China was mainly the result of the increased export of Chinese-made cotton yarn and piecegoods to relieve the needs of Southeast Asian countries under an arrangement of the American Commodity Aid Programme of 1948.[6] China's imports were dominated by relief goods from the U.S.A., while the bulk of its exports passed through Hong Kong, the only efficient centre of transhipment available. On the receiving side, the countries of Southeast Asia took an increasing share of Hong Kong's exports, 37·8%, 39·8% and 40·2% in 1946, 1947 and 1948, respectively. The ability of Hong Kong merchants to secure supplies of textiles in these years also offered them a great opportunity for establishing commercial relationships in new markets in the Middle East, South and East Africa. Far from being an entrepôt mainly for China, Hong Kong was looking now to wider horizons. When, as a result of the establishment of the Chinese Communist Government in 1949, Chinese manufactured goods were no longer exported, the time was ripe for Hong Kong to take over the role of workshop for its export trade partners.

A similar process of diversification was in progress in the shipping of the port. The policy of the Chinese Government to exclude foreign vessels from carrying cargoes and passengers between Chinese coastal stations and ports, and from proceeding up the Yangtze River beyond Woosung in Shanghai, forced Hong Kong-based shipping interests to turn their attention to trade between Japan, Korea and the Southeast Asian countries. There was a tendency for shipping companies, both foreign and Chinese, to move their offices from Shanghai to Hong Kong. Owing to the depletion of the merchant fleet during the war, however, the volume of shipping using the port was initially less than half the pre-war volume, and it was still 25% below this level in 1948.

TABLE 18.   VESSELS ENTERING AND CLEARING HONG KONG, 1946–9

Year	Number	Tonnage
1939	74,617	30,897,948
April 1946 – March 1947	46,547	13,869,490
April 1947 – March 1948	55,344	19,969,490
April 1948 – March 1949	66,815	23,040,126

SOURCE: Hong Kong, *Annual Report of the Director of Marine*, 1946–9.

The years 1949 and 1950 were a period of rapid political change in China which exercised a profound influence on commerce and shipping in the Far East and on the pattern of trade of the Colony. This change began at the end of 1948, with the southward advance of the Communist forces. The eclipse of trading activities followed the zone of military operations. Hong Kong's import and export services, however, were as much needed by the new regime as by the old during this period of national crisis, and the ports of North China under Communist control were reopened to trade with Hong Kong in the spring of 1949. By that time, Shanghai and the Yangtze Basin had been affected by war-created stagnation, the emergence from which was long delayed by the blockade imposed by Nationalist forces. Canton fell to the

Communists in October 1949 and, before the year was out, the change of regime in mainland China was completed. The major distortions in the movement of commodities enforced by circumstances in China were: the frequent arrival of essential exports from China by air in 1949; the maintenance of trade with Shanghai through Tientsin and Tsingtao, and the import by rail of goods direct from Shanghai; and the rise of Macao as a centre for transhipment and illicit trade.

Aviation was used on an increasing scale in the transport of cargoes. Overland routes in 1949 were inexpedient and often impossible. Tung oil and bristles were the main commodities brought to Hong Kong from Chungking by air. An alternative route was from Kunming to Haiphong by air, whence the freight was shipped to Hong Kong. This new air freight business, stimulated by the high value of essential goods in the civil war, remained and developed. It provided a useful service for developing new markets for the emerging local industries.

The dislocation of direct shipping to and from Shanghai made Tientsin the leading port in China, to which all Hong Kong trade with central and North China was directed. Nationalist guard-ships at the Yangtze estuary effectively sealed off Shanghai. The threat of air attacks from Taiwan bases deterred shipping at Amoy and Swatow, while the entrance to the Pearl River was also blocked. The risk to life and property involved in attempting calls at Chinese ports from Shanghai southwards barred coastal trade to all but the smallest craft. Practically all of China's import requirements were brought to Hong Kong for subsequent transhipment. Goods destined for Shanghai were shipped to Tientsin or Tsingtao, to continue their journey by rail. A small proportion went by rail over the Kowloon-Canton, and Canton-Hankow route. Correspondingly, the bulk of China's exports became imports to Hong Kong. For the first time in the history of the port, cargo was conveyed by rail between Hong Kong and Shanghai without transhipment at any point en route. The first through goods train from Shanghai arrived in Kowloon on 20 March 1950. Three more through train loads from Shanghai arrived in the following three months, but this railway traffic was suspended after the outbreak of the Korean War in June 1950. In any case, it was plain that when water transport became available once again the movement of goods between Hong Kong and Shanghai by railway could never be economic. Its use in 1950, however, indicates the part played by government activity in varying Hong Kong's hinterland.

Considerable confusion to Hong Kong's trade was caused by the large-scale smuggling between the Colony, Macao and China. The

Macao Government did not publish trade statistics, while the official Chinese trade returns (Maritime Customs) recorded hardly any trade between China and Macao. The trade and exchange restrictions imposed by the Chinese Government created the basis for the growth of an illicit trade from which officials, merchants and transport companies reaped rich profits. There being no exchange control in Macao such as existed in Hong Kong, there was always much diverting of Hong Kong export cargoes to Macao for re-export to the U.S.A. and other hard-currency countries. Macao was repeatedly used as a port of call by ocean steamers, which had to anchor far outside its harbour, for loading cargoes from Hong Kong that had been imported previously from various countries. Goods of Chinese origin were most prominent in this trade. Many Hong Kong merchants had found it expedient to make use of Macao to get their consignments to their destination. This disturbing factor in the entrepôt trade of Hong Kong persisted throughout the years 1949 and 1950.

Notwithstanding the tremendous odds, at times almost overwhelming, Hong Kong's merchants contrived to maintain their trade, changing their methods frequently to suit the situation and depending heavily on the combined geographical and political fact that Hong Kong was the only port on the China coast open to ocean-going shipping for a greater part of the year. China's foreign trade was reduced to a mere fraction of its potential but Hong Kong progressively monopolized this trade. The position of China in the trade of Hong Kong, which had been on the decline since the War, rose from 19·4% in 1948, to 23·2% in 1949 and 30·9% in 1950. If the recorded trade with Macao is also considered, as it should be, the percentages become 30 in 1949 and 35 in 1950.

Table 19 shows that by value Hong Kong's trade in 1950 was more than double that in 1948, the year when the Nationalist Government still controlled the greater part of China. Trade values were, however, much inflated by the high prices of commodities obtained in the China market. The main causes of high prices were the heavy demand in Shanghai after a long period when stocks were depleted as a result of the Nationalist blockade; the tendency to hoard commodities because of currency inflation; and the speculative value added to goods which had to break through the Nationalist blockade. A large discrepancy existed in local and Shanghai wholesale prices and traders were rewarded with outsize profits.

TABLE 19.   DIRECTION OF TRADE, HONG KONG, 1948–50
(VALUE IN MILLIONS HK$)

Country	1948		1949		1950	
	Value	%	Value	%	Value	%
China	710·8	19·4	1,178·2	23·2	2,319·0	30·9
Southeast Asia*	981·7	26·8	1,001·0	19·7	1,947·8	25·9
U.S.A.	539·8	14·7	809·8	15·9	963·8	12·8
United Kingdom	375·9	10·2	527·4	10·3	572·9	7·6
All others	1,052·0	28·9	1,552·6	30·9	1,699·7	22·8
Total	3,660·2	100	5,069·0	100	7,503·2	100

* Burma, Ceylon, Indo-China, India, Pakistan, Malaya, Philippines, Thailand and Indonesia.
SOURCE: *Hong Kong Trade Returns*, 1948–50.

Second to China, the U.S.A. maintained its position as a major source of supplies to Hong Kong, while Malaya came to be the leading market outside China for Hong Kong exports. Trade with Southeast Asian countries was going from strength to strength, although in the light of the inflated trade values in China, its rise seemed unspectacular. Japan, which disappeared from the trade of Hong Kong for over two years after the War, regained its pre-war position in 1950, taking 4·6% (HK$350 million) of the total.

As conditions in China settled down, at the end of 1949, the factors conducive to speculative trade were gradually replaced by harsher ones. In the period of consolidation of their power by the Communists, state enterprises grew rapidly. Private merchants were still permitted to practise, but were forced to curtail their activities because of unrealistic foreign exchange rates and because state control was tightened on the export of bristles, wood-oil, beans and bean-cake, which were the main sources of foreign exchange. A formidable array of official organizations and departments hampered trading activities, forcing the closure of foreign concerns in Tientsin and Shanghai. The old lines of business became impossible after April 1950. South China remained closed to sea-borne trade after the Communists took over Canton in October 1949, partly because of the Nationalist blockade and partly because the authorities in South China had no wish to meet foreign merchants half-way. In November 1949 103 ships of over sixty tons lay idle in the harbour of Hong Kong, an expression of the difficulty of trade with the Chinese ports.[7]

The outbreak of the Korean War in June 1950 brought a marked change. A boom in trade resulted from the large-scale buying by Communist government trade agencies and from the lively revival of the export of produce from China to secure foreign exchange. Import licences, which had previously been issued in China only for cargoes from the Communist bloc, were issued freely. Stocks in the warehouses of Hong Kong were quickly cleared and fresh orders were placed with suppliers abroad. Commodities in high demand were rubber and rubber manufactures, industrial chemicals, petroleum and petroleum products, transport equipment and parts, and machinery, including electrical appliances. Communist China's new attitude towards foreign trade coincided with the breakdown of the Nationalist blockade, which further improved the opportunities for trade. Hong Kong assumed the peculiar position of a warehouse for China where stocks of essential materials from all parts of the world were kept, awaiting dispatch. The Chinese Government, however, was paying dearly for this service. As evidence of the enhanced prices of commodities, Table 20 shows that goods handled in the port increased by 29·3% (1,611,176 tons) in 1950 while the total value of trade increased by 48·0% (HK$2,434 million).

TABLE 20. VOLUME OF TRADE, HONG KONG, 1948–51

Year	Total imported and exported cargo		Total value of trade	
	tons	*% change*	*HK$ million*	*% change*
1948	4,098,028	—	3,660	—
1949	5,494,963	+34·0%	5,069	+38·5%
1950	7,106,139	+29·3%	7,503	+48·0%
1951	5,871,183	−17·3%	9,303	+23·9%

SOURCE: Szczepanik, E., *The Economic Growth of Hong Kong*, 1958, p. 157.

The final and most radical change occurred when, as a result of the participation of Communist China in the Korean War, an embargo on the export of strategic goods to China, including Hong Kong, was enforced by the U.S.A. in December 1950 followed by the United Nations restriction to the same effect in May 1951. The U.S. embargo immediately led to the off-loading in the Philippines and other countries of cargoes on their way to Hong Kong. The value of imports to Hong Kong from the U.S.A. fell from HK$655·3 million in 1950 to HK$373·5 million in 1951, while exports from Hong Kong to the U.S.A. fell from

HK$308·7 million to HK$162·5 million. Table 20 brings out the remarkable fact that in 1951, while the volume of cargo handled at the port decreased by 17·3%, the total value of trade increased by 23·9%. This discrepancy is explained by inflated prices and changes in the purchasing power of money.[8] After the announcement of the U.S. embargo, excessively high prices were demanded and paid in the knowledge that supplies sold might be difficult to replace in the future. Up to the month of May 1951, of the new orders for goods for eventual consumption in China, a high proportion was placed in European countries. The United Nations embargo order, however, closed all normal sources of supply after May 1951. By way of retaliation, the Chinese Government announced their policy of allowing exports only when they were covered by imports of commodities, and of the restriction of imports to a specified list of goods, the majority of which were taken from the United Nations embargo list. Trade in the few non-strategic commodities still permissible under the embargo order was thus further restricted by the Chinese demand. This shook the entrepôt economy of Hong Kong to its foundations—and a radical change was needed for it to survive.

Development of Port Facilities and Town Planning

Progress in the post-war rehabilitation of port facilities was slow, owing to the world-wide shortage of construction materials. The greater part of the energy and resources of the Colony was devoted to the rehabilitation of housing. This is not to say, however, that the efficiency of the port fell to any great extent. A comparison of the volume of shipping using the port before and after the war shows the effects of the slow recovery of port facilities on the prosperity of the port.

Table 21 demonstrates that the volume of post-war shipping engaged in foreign trade, for which particular berthing and mechanical equipment might be needed, was only 38% of the pre-war level. The total volume of shipping of all classes was 36% of what it had been. This vastly-reduced demand for services in the port was no doubt sufficiently met by the existing facilities, after quick repairs had been made to stop further deterioration. Private companies were making heavy capital outlays in the transformation and renovation of harbour craft, gear and buildings. A conservative estimate put the figure of post-war capital expenditure of wharf and godown companies, shipbuilding and ship-repair yards, oil-bunkering companies, and ferry and steamer companies at HK$125,000,000.[9] This figure does not include profits ploughed back into local businesses, financing by banks or investment by smaller companies.

TABLE 21. SHIPPING ENTERED AND CLEARED, 1939 AND 1946

Class of vessels	1939		1946		Change	
	no.	tonnage	no.	tonnage	no.	tonnage
FOREIGN TRADE						
Ocean-going	7,407	22,148,228	3,147	8,136,189	−14,102	−14,012,039
River steamer	7,614	6,692,338	1,504	1,027,936	−6,110	−5,664,402
Steamer under 60 tons	960	32,837	3,451	89,881	+2,491	+57,004
Junks	7,900	323,063	29,820	1,734,764	+21,920	+1,411,701
Total foreign trade	23,881	29,196,466	37,922	10,988,770	+14,041	−18,207,696
LOCAL TRADE						
Steamers over 60 tons	124	29,933	—	—	−124	−29,933
Steam launches	24,847	804,776	2,242	117,383	−22,605	−687,393
Junks	25,765	866,773	5,320	138,158	−20,445	−728,615
Grand total	74,617	30,897,948	45,484	11,244,311	−29,133	−19,653,637
						net decrease

SOURCE: Hong Kong, *Annual Report of the Director of Marine*, 1946–7; Hong Kong Government, *Annual Report*, 1947.

Two interesting points about the changes in the nature of shipping are, firstly, a large increase in the number but a decrease in the tonnage of vessels employed in foreign trade and, secondly, a large decrease in the number of launches in local trade. The first change indicates a widespread employment of junks in foreign trade. They were mainly engaged on the China coast to make up for the depleted fleet of coasting steamers. The coasting trade was also more restricted than it had been before the War and not many river or coasting steamers found it sufficiently remunerative to keep running. A number of the junks had been mechanized for this purpose. In view of the limited means of coastal transport they were not interfered with, although their fitting out was far below safety requirements. The second change reflects a rather serious setback in the efficiency of the operation of the port in that the loss of steam launches in local waters hampered the stevedoring service and internal communications. There were only thirteen ferries engaged in maintaining communications between Hong Kong and Kowloon and the outlying districts and islands in 1948, as compared with forty before the war. Before building material and machinery were made available to local shipyards, the operation of the port depended on the seventy vessels, consisting of tugs, launches and lighters, sold to Hong Kong by the Ministry of Transport in 1946. Reconditioning work on these and on vessels that survived the War was done in local shipyards.

During the reconstruction period, the opportunity was taken to modernize plant and equipment where these needed replacement, to increase mechanization and to prepare for a broader range of assignments. New types of navigation lights inside the harbour and along its approaches were installed. Mooring-buoys were replaced by improved models made of cast steel which had a considerably greater breaking strength than their predecessors.

From 1949 on new additions were made to port facilities. A quarantine anchorage was opened at Kowloon Bay to supplement the one at the western end of the harbour. It was intended for the convenience of vessels entering the harbour by the eastern entrance and to reduce the number of crossings of east-west and north-south traffic in the harbour. A new wharf was completed in this year by the Hong Kong and Kowloon Wharf and Godown Company at the northern end of their premises in Kowloon. In 1950, at North Point, a new company completed the only commercial deep-water berth on the Island of Hong Kong. The new company, which operated under the management of the long-established China Provident Loan and Mortgage Company, provided a quayage of 1,223 linear feet, of which 800 could accommodate vessels drawing up to thirty feet of water. Storage space was made available for 20,000 measurement tons. Since the end of the War, the public warehouse companies had taken over the premises of many private godowns at Kennedy Town and at West Point, besides redeveloping their original buildings. From a storage capacity of just over 300,000 measurement tons (m. tons) left by the Japanese occupation, covered godown space increased to 700,000 m. tons in 1947, to 888,130 m. tons in 1948, and to 900,000 m. tons in 1949. No census of privately-owned godowns was taken but the 1950 estimate was 450,000 m. tons.[10] Special warehousing for oil products, tobacco and sugar provided for a further 200,000 m. tons. These figures include many of the store rooms of firms engaged in the import and export of Chinese produce, where cargo-handling facilities did not exist. The overall capacity in 1950 was just over $1\frac{1}{2}$ million m. tons of which 932,300 m. tons were controlled by the three main companies: the Hong Kong and Kowloon Wharf and Godown Company, Holt's Wharf, and the China Provident Loan and Mortgage Company, with their associated North Point Wharves.

Reclamation, which had been responsible for most of the changes in the outline of the harbour, was resumed soon after the War. It was carried out on a much smaller scale, since the financial and technical resources of the Colony were directed to more pressing needs such as the reconstruction of buildings, the improvement of public utilities, urban water supply and the recuperation of agriculture and fisheries. The early resumption of reclamation resulted from the need to provide places for disposal of rubble from building reconstruction. Similar dumps were required to accommodate the spoil obtained from dredging the harbour. The Government delineated areas of spoil disposal at North Point, Cheung Sha Wan, Hung Hom and Kennedy Town. The last-named location was rapidly filled and dumping had to be stopped, pending a further extension of the seawall to hold back the debris. Kwun Tong became the largest area for reclamation by dumping as it received spoil regularly from dredging in the harbour. No dredging had been done during the Japanese occupation with the result that considerable silting had occurred alongside seawalls and at sewer and storm-water outfalls. Large quantities of spoil were obtained while clearing the harbour of this silting. Dredging was also needed to clear foundations for the seawall extension. The post-war building boom, that began in 1948, continued the dumping of debris from new site formation. At North Point there was a race between the extension of the seawall and the filling in of the area behind, in the years 1947–50. Preliminary work on three major reclamation schemes at Victoria Central, Hung Hom and Kwun Tong was started in 1947. The reclamation at Victoria Central was an ambitious project which sought to provide an additional strip of land along the whole of the waterfront of Victoria from the Naval Dockyard to Possession Point. Little development occurred at Hung Hom and Kwun Tong before 1950.

The greatest of all changes in the outline of the harbour resulted from the decision to provide an international airport. Although the new runway, which now forms the most conspicuous landmark in the harbour plan, took shape in the 1950s, work leading to its formation was begun as early as 1946. The two major factors that urged the construction of the new airport were the inadequacy of the Japanese-constructed airstrips to accommodate the modern long-range aircraft then in use, and the prospect of the Colony becoming a centre of aviation for the whole area of Southeast Asia, instead of serving as a mere feeder-aerodrome for other centres.

It has been generally accepted that the prosperity of the port was based on efficient communications. With the post-war development of air transport, the increasing proportion of air passengers to sea passengers indicated the danger of relying solely on land and water transport. The provision of an international airport would improve the position of Hong Kong as a hub of communication in the Far East. Besides attracting foreign visitors and businessmen, who would otherwise by-pass Hong Kong, it would increase the mobility of the local merchants and speed up transactions. On the other hand, it was probable that, by leaving Kai Tak as it was, Hong Kong would be without an effective airport altogether when the restricted service it could provide was no longer acceptable to the new types of aircraft being developed. There being no British alternative to Hong Kong on the main air routes in the area, the loss of Hong Kong as an international airport was also seen to be a potential weakness in the bargaining power of the British Government in civil aviation negotiations.[11]

The sheltering ranges of hills around the urban area, which contributed to Hong Kong's fine harbour, proved to be a great obstacle to airport development (Fig. 15). Detailed investigations were made of several proposed sites all over the Colony, at Deep Bay, Stonecutters Island,

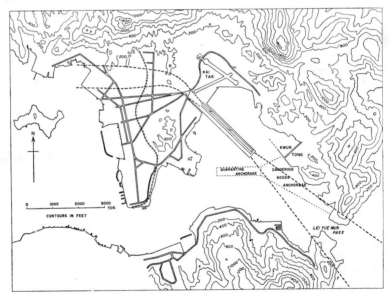

Figure 15. Approaches to Kai Tak airport in relation to relief.

Stanley and the old site of Kai Tak. For technical and financial reasons all of these were abandoned in favour of building a promontory into Kowloon Bay. An area of about 170 acres, released from the old airport, provided scope for redevelopment. As early as 1948, town planners were considering Kai Tak as 'the possible future satellite' and 'the most suitable and easily developed site, for a short-term policy, to eliminate overcrowding from Hong Kong and Kowloon.'[12]

Planning was characteristic of urban development in the post-war years. The Town Planning Office of Hong Kong, established in April 1947, benefited immensely from the expert advice of Sir Patrick Abercrombie, who visited the Colony in November 1947. The recommendations put forward in his Report of September 1948 later formed the basis of a detailed survey and future planning. The difficulties confronting town planners in Hong Kong were seen by Sir Patrick to be related to two characteristic problems: firstly, the shortage of land for any sort of urban expansion and, secondly, an unlimited reservoir of possible immigration. 'The combined presence of these two characteristics does indeed produce something like a unique result.'[13] Reclamation continued to be the solution to the first problem while, for the second, an 'ultimate population' was to be maintained by artificial restriction. A figure of two million was regarded as the maximum for the population. The Colony was seen to be faced with the alternatives of a larger population or a better standard of living.

Among the important aspects of general planning to which attention was directed were: the location of industries in the correct zones by type, i.e. intermediate, light, home or domestic and noxious; the preservation of open space; the correct siting of housing; the control of the growing density of population; and the prevention of piecemeal reconstruction. Although it had been stressed that no final and definite plan was attempted and that the report was necessarily limited to general suggestions, some of the ideas therein were implemented as far as could be justified by the economic position of the Colony. Among the developments since realized, which directly affected the movement of shipping and cargo in the port, were the reclamations at Hong Kong Island, Kowloon and the New Territories (Tsuen Wan and Kwai Chung); the shifting of the typhoon anchorage at Causeway Bay; the removal of the Naval Dockyard from the heart of the city; and the provision of traffic arteries running the length of the city of Victoria and the Kowloon peninsula. Indirectly, activities in the port were affected by a movement towards decentralization, that is, the provision of jobs, accommodation

and amenities in industrial zones in suburban districts and in the New
Territories. Recognizing the fundamental fact that the Colony was an
entrepôt port, the preliminary planning Report had provided for the
construction of new piers, the re-alignment of the railway and the
provision of a road and railway link across the harbour (Fig. 16).
However, the sudden change in the direction of the economic development of Hong Kong, soon after the visit of Sir Patrick Abercrombie,
called for a slower approach to the development of port facilities.

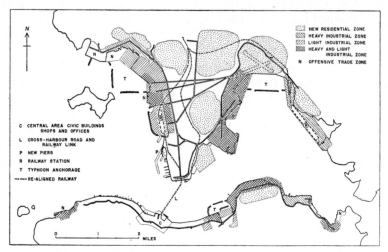

Figure 16. Preliminary planning of Hong Kong, 1948.

Based on an estimated population of one and a half million in 1948, the
Report was made at a time when the post-war movement of people,
most of whom were returning pre-war immigrants, had diminished. It
took into consideration the prevalent 'economic immigration'[14] of
Chinese industries and people. No forecast could have been made,
however, of the mass influx of people in 1949 which followed the political
and economic changes on the mainland. At the peak of this wave of
immigration in September and October 1949, total arrivals in Hong
Kong numbered over 10,000 per week. By May 1950, there was an
increase in population of some 700,000 'political refugees', in addition
to the 'economic immigration' between the end of the war and 1949.
A number of these returned to China when conditions settled, yet, by
April 1950, the population figure of the Colony had risen to 2,360,000.
It was plain that such an alarming rate of increase had to be checked.

The Immigration Control Ordinance, introduced in 1940 but withheld in 1945, was reinforced in 1949 and put into effect in April 1950. Despite this control, new immigrants were still arriving at the rate of 20,000 to 25,000 a year. 'The very face of Hong Kong underwent a rapid and ugly change',[15] as a result of the development of squatter areas.[16] Planners found themselves more and more engaged in immediate problems of accommodation, water supply, education and public health.

Industrialization

The industrial development of Hong Kong before 1947 could well be used to illustrate the inevitable situation of ports which become industrial centres by virtue of their location at break-of-bulk points, or at points of minimum procurement cost, and by virtue of their function as large population centres. The established industries before 1947 were of a type which might suitably be described as general port industries,[17] operating with no great amount of heavy material and requiring no special handling facilities for raw materials or for products. Such industries included flour-milling, vegetable-oil refining, sugar-refining, the processing of foodstuffs, rubber-consuming industries, the manufacture of paint and varnish, tobacco processing, and tanning. Exceptions to general port industries were the shipbuilding and ship-repairing industries and cement work, in which a fair amount of special port installation had to be provided along with an extensive area for works, storage and dumps. Industries which were not necessarily related to port functions but which were attracted to the large population centre were the textile industries, the manufacture of matches and rattan ware, printing, and the manufacture of a wide range of household utensils.

The rapid industrialization after 1947 coincided with a period when factors of production were particularly favourable. Towards the end of 1946, Chinese manufacturers, especially Shanghai industrialists, became increasingly concerned about the future. Political and economic conditions within China were rapidly deteriorating and the policy of its Government towards private industry was uncertain. On the other hand, there existed in Hong Kong a number of factors attractive to industry: peace and security under a stable government; a deep-rooted tradition of efficiency in such services as banking, shipping and insurance; a large merchant community with commercial links all over the world; a simple faith in the advantages of free enterprise and minimum interference by the Government in trade or industry; membership of the sterling area; the existence of an open exchange market; a stable currency; preference in Commonwealth markets; and an abundant labour force, relatively free from industrial disputes. It is true that these factors by themselves were insufficient to loose the flood of capital and entrepreneurial skill that accounted for the industrialization of the Colony. It was their absence from industry within China that generated the inter-regional movement so vital to the growth of new centres of production.

A review of the conditions of industry before 1947 throws light on the scale of development during the following years. The immediate task of the Colony in 1945 and 1946 was the rehabilitation of its main source of income, the entrepôt trade. The heavier industries associated with shipping were thus the first to recover. Until 1948 the shipbuilding and ship-repairing industries were the major sources of industrial employment, taking 28% of all registered workers. At the end of 1946, the shipyards were working at only 30–40% pre-war capacity and employing 5,000–7,000 workers in ten shipyards as against 12,000 to 15,000 workers employed before the War. There was much more work than could be handled, for, in addition to repairs, reconversion work of all types was required by many vessels which had been adapted to special uses during the War. The lack of constructional material, however, prevented the full resumption of operations.

The manufacturing industries were faced with a more serious shortage of raw materials. The greatest burden fell on the textile industries, which had been the leading industries before the War, with 150 factories engaged in weaving and 450 in knitting, employing 25,000 and 15,000 workers respectively. At the end of 1946, the first post-war shipment of yarn arrived from Japan, putting ninety cotton-weaving factories into operation, but the knitting factories were still idle. An additional obstacle to the recovery of this industry was the depreciation of machinery, which was estimated as 50%.

Rubber shoes were produced before the War at the rate of twenty million pairs a year. The biggest factory employed 3,000 workers and there were nine others employing about 10,000 in aggregate. A number of small factories had grown up after the War. By the end of 1946, about 6,000 people were employed on production at 20–25% of the pre-war level. In the manufacture of torches and batteries, 20 factories employed 2,000 to 3,000 workers before the War, but only ten factories resumed operation in 1946, with 400 to 600 workers producing at 20% of pre-war capacity. The food-processing industries constituted a main branch in the labour-absorbing industries before the War. The post-war rise in the cost of production and the scarcity of foodstuffs affected different food-processing factories in varying degrees. On average, production was reduced to from 10 to 40% of the pre-war level. No assessment can be made of the changes in the minor industries of the Colony but, according to observations made by the United Kingdom Board of Trade Mission to China in late 1946,[18] the general level of industrial activity in Hong Kong was 20% of the pre-war capacity. There were 260 factories in operation as compared with 1,250 in 1941.

The textile industries which had adapted to the abundant supply of unskilled labour in post-war years, claimed the attention of both official and private interests. Demand being large, no serious consideration was given to working conditions and efficient operation. With the assistance of the government Supplies, Trade and Industry Department, more cotton yarn was made available from Japan and China by the end of 1946. In November 1946, the Revised Temporary Foreign Trade Regulations of the Chinese Government came into effect, and the textile industries, prepared for the full-scale resumption of work, were again held back. By June 1947, cotton weavers were working at only 10–20% of capacity. The tightening of government control in China, however set off the flow of industrial enterprise into Hong Kong. The most significant of the developments in 1947 was the establishment of two modern cotton-spinning plants, the first in the Colony. Machinery for these plants, ordered towards the end of the War in the United Kingdom and the U.S.A., was on its way to Shanghai via Hong Kong. Shipment was held so long at Hong Kong, waiting for the improvement of political and economic conditions in China, that it was eventually decided to put the plants to work within the security of the Colony. This, coupled with the fact that capital was readily available, led to an ambitious expansion of the textile industries.

Favourable conditions returned during the last quarter of 1947, with prices rising in the world market while local production costs declined. A further spur was given when the Japanese exports decreased, as a result of the stipulation of the occupying authority that textiles from that country could be bought only in exchange for U.S. dollars. With production in the local weaving industries rising, the demand for yarn seemed insatiable. Two spinning mills, operating 7,500 spindles each, went into production early in 1948. Plans were immediately made for setting up two further mills of 15,000 and 25,000 spindles each. It was not fully realized, however, that the delivery of machinery was subject to delays. In the event, much of the machinery ordered subsequently arrived at the stage when the shortage of cotton yarn was beginning to be satisfied and competition was building up. Nonetheless, the two spinning mills were a remarkable advance in the modernization of the textile industries of Hong Kong. Their example was soon followed by their competitors. It was found that local workers did not possess sufficient knowledge to make efficient use of the new machinery and Shanghai workers were encouraged to come in. The following table shows the development of the spinning industry in the years 1948–50.

TABLE 22. DEVELOPMENT OF THE SPINNING INDUSTRY, 1948–50

	1948	*1949*	*1950*
Number of mills	5	11	13
Spindles (thousands)	88	132	187·5
Year's output (million lbs.)	6·5	23·7	54·0

SOURCE: *The Hong Kong Exporter and Far Eastern Importer,* 1958–9.

This local source of yarn had lowered the cost of production to weavers before the end of 1948. However, Chinese yarns were competing strongly under the export drive of the Chinese Government. Local spinners were urged to develop overseas markets where quality was sought. Owing to the tight financial conditions, ready cash had to be found by diverting some of the output to local weavers at unremunerative prices. A number of the spinners were induced to consider going into the weaving business themselves, in order to ensure the regular absorption of a proportion of their output.

In the weaving industry, post-war rehabilitation was completed by the end of 1947. Following a brief period of thriving business in 1947–8, the weavers met strong competition from China and also from Japan, which was regaining a large share of the Southeast Asian market. Many firms were compelled to modernize their plant to bring their cost of production into line with world prices and to maintain standards of production. As a result of the growth of the spinning and weaving industries, those industries which provided the finishing services, namely the bleaching and dyeing mills and the garment industries, were firmly established by 1950.

The process of modernization spread to other industries which had long been established in the Colony and which had to compete in overseas markets. At the same time, the development of new industries, some of which were transplanted from Shanghai, continued. The most prominent among these were the manufacture of plastic ware, aluminium ware, enamelware and electrical goods. A new addition to the heavy industries of the Colony was the ship-breaking industry, which owed its initial development to the port. Starting with three firms in 1947, Hong Kong had grown to be the leading ship-breaking centre in the world by 1959.[19] The Pacific War left a large number of wrecks in the harbour which had to be disposed of. These were turned into the raw material of the industry, the end product of which found ready markets in a world short of building materials. This industry required very little skilled labour and operated at low overhead costs, since it was possible to substitute the abundant supply of cheap labour for mechanical handling. It had an advantage over other heavy industries in that no land site was required for the erection of a factory or workshop. Special water sites were needed for the beaching of ships under demolition but, before the industry had grown to its full size, such water sites were easily obtainable in the harbour. The products of this industry were taken up by local steel-rolling mills, which made profitable use of the scrap in their own works, and turned out mild steel bars which found a ready market in local construction work. The industry also supplied the local shipyards when steel from other sources was not available but, like all other new industries in the Colony, it had developed markets in overseas countries, especially in Japan.

Table 23 illustrates the growth of industry in the first phase of the post-war industrialization of the Colony. These figures, which represent workers in registered and recorded factories only, do not give a complete picture of the industrial community. The number of workers employed in workshops and family concerns not qualified for registration probably exceeded that which came under the supervision of the Commissioner of Labour.[20]

TABLE 23. WORKERS EMPLOYED IN REGISTERED AND RECORDED FACTORIES
AND WORKSHOPS, 1947–51

	1947	1948	1949	1950	1951
Number of concerns	978	1,137	1,284	1,525	1,788
Number of employees	51,627	61,714	65,271	89,512	93,837

SOURCE: Hong Kong, *Report of the Commissioner of Labour,* 1947–51.

Following a tremendous upsurge in 1949, when the inflow of capital and people from China was specially strong, industrial development suffered a setback in 1950, largely as the result of the speculative trade boom absorbing large proportions of available capital. Strong competition was felt from cheap Japanese products, which had been fighting their way back into the Southeast Asian markets for more than a year. Upon the announcement of the United States embargo on the export of strategic materials to China, including Hong Kong, many factories immediately found themselves without supplies since shortage of capital meant that they did not keep stocks of raw materials. Production was interrupted for several months before the U.S. Government modified the restrictions, on the provision of guarantees by the Hong Kong Government regarding the end use of U.S. material processed in the Colony. Merchants also turned quickly to other sources of supply. The Hong Kong Government, which had hitherto played a passive part in the industrial development of the Colony, began to take a keen interest in the welfare of this potential source of revenue. In December 1950, a survey of monthly factory requirements was made, and on the basis of this, the Essential Supplies Certificates System was introduced to facilitate the procurement of raw materials. A series of import and export controls, movement controls and end-use controls were enforced. The United Nations embargo that followed in June 1951 extended the restrictions to all sources of supply to Hong Kong. Government action then became vital to the survival of the local industries. At this early stage of industrialization, therefore, the prosperity of the Colony continued to be swayed by forces outside its own control.

CHAPTER SIX

MODERNIZATION OF THE PORT, 1951–70

For the port of Hong Kong, the United Nations embargo on trade with mainland China amounted to the loss of its traditional hinterland. The reorientation of the port's economy required the complete readjustment of its trading activities. China's share of the export trade of Hong Kong was reduced from 36·2% in 1951 to 18·3% in 1952, and it continued to dwindle to the relatively insignificant amount of 0·5% in 1967. Imports from China, on the other hand, were maintained at about one-quarter to one-fifth of the total imports into Hong Kong, increasing in absolute value with the growth of the overall trade. This growth is explained by the fact that Hong Kong is largely dependent on China for its supply of food, especially live animals, fruit, vegetables and other perishables. The trade with China is thus one-sided, with a heavy balance in favour of China.

The sharp fall in the trade with China entailed a change in the pattern of shipping in the port. The decline in the tonnage of cargo handled in the port amounted to 1·4 million (22%) in the year 1951–2, a loss borne mainly by imports from the U.S.A. and exports to China, though the former revived gradually in subsequent years with the relaxation of controls, while the latter continued to decline. Considerable reductions in the activities of river steamers and in junk traffic were recorded between 1952 and 1956. Since 1956, this traffic has fluctuated from year to year but, overall, it has declined during the decade ending in 1970 (Table 24). European and Chinese owners of Hong Kong-based vessels, developed further 'near-seas'[1] routes including those to the Bay of Bengal, the Straits, Bangkok, Saigon, Borneo, the Philippines, Formosa, Korea and Japan. The river-steamer traffic, like the export trade to China, never revived, despite improvements in the entrepôt trade with China in the late 1950s. Wherever possible, the Chinese Government pursued a policy of barter trade, chartering vessels and ordering for direct shipment to Chinese ports such as Tientsin, Tsingtao, Shanghai and Whampoa, thus by-passing Hong Kong. This method of trade was particularly suited to the Chinese Government's bulk-buying policy. Hong Kong was left to handle a wide range of minor commodities which could only be obtained piecemeal by small merchants.[2]

TABLE 24.   CARGOES CARRIED BY RIVER STEAMERS, LAUNCHES AND JUNKS IN THE
EXTERNAL TRADE OF HONG KONG, 1950–70 (IN D.W. TONS)

Year	Imports		Exports	
	River steamers	*Launches and junks*	*River steamers*	*Launches and junks*
1950–1	84,036	435,382	89,410	167,461
1951–2	34,841	510,100	75,870	123,341
1955–6	12,379	782,675	18,291	74,403
1956–7	14,383	1,103,679	19,942	118,283
1960–1	13,035	1,000,371	18,188	133,526
1961–2	11,726	1,052,408	17,662	203,282
1965–6	5,917	2,020,433	8,741	155,802
1966–7	8,149	1,913,849	7,131	121,022
1969–70	14,511	1,190,586	6,306	149,709

SOURCE: Hong Kong, *Annual Report of the Director of Marine*, 1969–70.

The transfer of shipping activities to 'near-seas' routes was complementary to the development of the Southeast Asian markets for Hong
Kong-manufactured goods. The raw materials required and the products
turned out by local industries took an ever-increasing share of the
cargoes for shipping, which in turn provided ready access to the sources
of supply and to markets. From a transhipment port in which most
cargoes handled were in transit, Hong Kong had changed to a destination
port incorporating much of the role of its hinterland.[3] The physical
contraction of the hinterland made it imperative that the traffic of the
port should come from the exchange of goods between the surrounding
countries and between these and countries further abroad. Tremendous
efforts were made to promote the sale not only of the products of Hong
Kong but also of commercial services and of the local merchants' expert
knowledge of world and particularly regional markets. A new form of
entrepôt trade, involving all the countries of the Far East, developed as
these countries began to use Hong Kong as an intermediary for the
purchase of goods from all over the world, and for the sale of their own
products.

The years 1952–5 marked a period of adjustment from a commercial
economy to one dominated by industry. Since 1955, there has been a
continued upswing in the prosperity of the port as the increase in the
value of trade, in the tonnage of shipping entering and clearing the port,
and in the tonnage of cargoes imported and exported bear witness

(Table 29). The 1951 boom value of trade was exceeded in 1960, while cargoes handled in foreign trade showed an improvement of 1,072,749 tons over the peak of 1951. It is important to note, however, that the pre-war figure for the tonnage of ocean-going vessels using the port was regained only after 1957. This fact must be considered when studying the efficiency of the present port and the efforts put into developing its facilities.

Since it has become the major function of the port to serve its industries, it is important to note that industrial development in the last two decades has been achieved mainly in light industries. This largely explains the nature of the cargo handled and the stevedoring practices employed. There is no bulk-cargo traffic, with the exception of fuel, the transport of which is entirely in the hands of the oil companies, both physically and operationally detached from the port proper. The only addition to pre-war heavy industry has been ship-breaking, with its associated steel-rolling mills. This addition, however, has had little effect on the nature of the port's cargoes since the raw material—ships for the demolition yards—comes in afloat, while a major part of the produce is consumed locally.

Recent Trade Pattern

The predominance of general cargo in the trade of Hong Kong is shown in Table 25. Imports, domestic exports and re-exports in the year 1970 accounted for 54%, 38% and 8% respectively of the total trade by value. The separate recording of re-exports and domestic exports, a system adopted since 1959, has made it possible to ascertain the role of the entrepôt trade. In 1961 the value of re-exports was 16·6% of the value of imports, while in 1967 this had increased to 19·9% and again fallen to 16·6% in 1970.[4] A new type of entrepôt trade has evolved, unlike the former which was geared to the re-export of Chinese goods. Since 1963, manufactured goods have dominated the commodity pattern of re-exports. Commodities of which a high proportion is imported for re-export are textiles and textile fibres, non-metallic mineral manufactures especially precious stones, medicinal and pharmaceutical products, chemicals and miscellaneous manufactured articles. Table 26 underlines the fact that the entrepôt services of Hong Kong are still widely used by the neighbouring countries of Southeast Asia. Three countries, Japan, Singapore and Indonesia, have been the largest buyers since 1964. Despite the changes in its foreign trade policy, China is still using Hong Kong as a trading post for the sale of its foodstuffs, textile yarn, fabrics

TABLE 25. TRADE OF HONG KONG, COMMODITY PATTERN BY MAIN GROUPS, 1970

	Imports	Re-exports		Domestic exports
	% of total	% of total		% of total
Manufactured goods	33	41	Clothing	35
Food and live animals	17	11	Miscellaneous manufactured articles	25
Machinery and transport equipment	16	10	Electrical machinery	10
Miscellaneous manufactured articles	12	12	Textile yarn, fabrics and made-up articles	10
Chemicals	8	17	Manufactures of metal	3
Crude materials, inedible, except fuels	8	6	Footwear	2

SOURCE: Hong Kong Government, *Annual Report,* 1970.

and made-up articles, crude animal and vegetable material, the chief
outlets for which are Southeast Asian countries. Re-export of goods
originating from China amounted to 24% of all re-exports in 1970.
For the Hong Kong merchants, the profits of this entrepôt trade have
been nothing compared with those of the pre-Korean War years because
there is little sorting or re-packing required for these Chinese commodities.

TABLE 26. PRINCIPAL MARKETS FOR HONG KONG'S RE-EXPORTS, 1970

By country	% of all re-exports	By continent and Commonwealth countries	% of all re-exports
Japan	20	Asia	62
Singapore	12	Western Europe	12
U.S.A.	8	North America	9
Indonesia	7	Africa	6
Taiwan	5	Commonwealth countries	26
Republic of Korea	3		
Belgium & Luxembourg	3		

SOURCE: Hong Kong Government, *Annual Report,* 1970.

As the principal supplier of food, China was the main source of Hong
Kong's imports, until 1968 when Japan took the lead. In marked
contrast to this is Hong Kong's trade with the U.S.A., which has
supplanted China as Hong Kong's leading trade partner, taking 42%

of domestic exports and 8% of re-exports, while supplying 13% of imports in 1970. The corresponding figures for the U.K. are 12%, 3% and 9%, respectively.

TABLE 27. VALUE OF EXPORTS OF HONG KONG PRODUCTS (HK$ MILLIONS)

	1950	*1952*	*1957*	*1959*	*1965*	*1970*
Exports of H.K. products	196·6	486·2	1,202·0	2,282·1	5,026·8	12,346·5
Percentage of total exports	5·3%	16·7%	39·8%	69·6%	76·9%	81·0%
Total exports	3,715·6	2,899·0	3,016·3	3,277·5	6,529·5	15,238·0

SOURCES: *Far Eastern Economic Review, XXIV*, No. 4; *Commerce, Industry, Finance Directory*, Hong Kong, 1961; Hong Kong Government, *Annual Report*, 1965, 1970.

In the export trade, produce from local factories provides an increasing share of the cargoes carried. In 1950, when the external trade of Hong Kong was dominated by China, only 5·3% of the exports were of Hong Kong origin. This figure rose to 42·1% in 1958, 77·3% in 1961 and 81% in 1970. The significance of this change is greater than the figures suggest because the value of every dollar of domestic produce is worth many times the same value of re-exports in terms of employment and national income. The industries of Hong Kong have not been developed to serve the local market. The majority of the 3·9 million local people belong to the lower-income groups, for whom China often floods the market with extraordinarily cheap products. The volume

TABLE 28. DESTINATION OF EXPORT OF HONG KONG PRODUCTS

	1956 %	*1957* %	*1958* %	*1963* %	*1967* %	*1970* %
Asian areas	40	31	25	21	14	12
United Kingdom	23	23	26	23	17	12
Africa	15	17	13	7	4	4
America	12	18	23	30	43	45
Europe*	3	5	7	12	14	17
Oceania	6	6	6	5	5	5

* Western Europe excluding U.K.

SOURCES: Hong Kong, *Annual Report of the Director of Commerce and Industry*, 1958–9, and 1963–4; Review of Overseas Trade in 1967, Hong Kong; *Hong Kong Monthly Digest of Statistics*, March 1971.

and direction of the export of Hong Kong goods are influenced by many factors, among the more important of which are the varying degrees of Commonwealth Preference; the purchasing power of its markets; the growth of industries in developing countries; quota restrictions; and tariffs. In recent years, the attempts to develop markets where quality rather than low price is sought are demonstrated by the swing from Asia towards European and North American countries, as Table 28 shows.

The Changing Configuration of the Port

Throughout the history of the port, the shortage of land has continued to be a major problem in its development. The conflicting claims on space within the harbour area by industry and port development are complicated by the need to accommodate the anticipated annual increase of an additional 100,000 or more people, and an indefinite number of immigrants. As outlined in previous chapters, the encroachment of land into the harbour has been an accepted process. The rapidity with which reclamation has been carried out in the last decade, however, has given rise to the observation that the time will soon come when the harbour will not be able to accommodate all the ships that wish to use it.[5] The Kai Tak airport development in 1954–6 ended the use of Kowloon Bay as a typhoon refuge for ships under repair at the Hong Kong and Whampoa Docks and has reduced the sizes of the quarantine and dangerous goods anchorages in the eastern part of the harbour. The ship-breaking industry, for which ideal sites coincided with the best sites for reclamation, has been forced to leave all the early sites at Cheung Sha Wan and Ngau Tau Kok and to develop the difficult site at Junk Bay, outside the harbour.[6]

On Hong Kong Island, three major reclamations were completed in the years 1951–3 (Fig. 17). The waterfront on the southern side of the harbour was straightened where these reclamations were carried out. At North Point, an area of 5·3 acres was made available for small factories and a large housing estate. The Causeway Bay reclamation provided fifty-five acres of land which was entirely devoted to recreational purposes. The designation of this extensive area for use as a public park was influenced by the Abercrombie Report on planning, which laid much stress on the preservation of open space. As a result of this reclamation, the typhoon shelter was displaced 140 yards further north, towards the centre of the harbour, and the opportunity was taken to enlarge it to provide sixty-five acres of sheltered water to accommodate the increasing number of small craft. The Central Reclamation Scheme

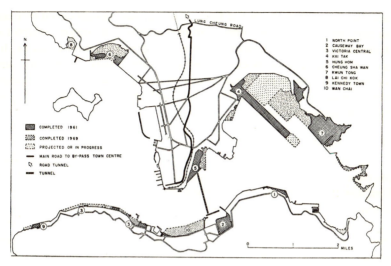

Figure 17. Post-war development of Hong Kong harbour.

was devoted to public amenities. This development had been inspired by the criticism in the Abercrombie Report that 'Hong Kong is perhaps more deficient in public buildings than any other town of comparable size in the world.'[7]

In compliance with the recommendations of the Report, work was started in 1954 to remove the hill at Ma Tau Kok to reclaim the waterfront, making six acres of land for a concourse for a new ferry pier (the Kowloon City Ferry Pier). With the rise in demand for industrial land, reclamation work at Kwun Tong was put in hand. This area ceased to be a refuse dump in 1955 and obtained fill from excavation of the adjacent hills. Designed to be a new town of 300,000 people and the biggest single area of light industries within the harbour area, Kwun Tong provided 641 acres of land, of which 154 acres were solely for industries and 239 acres for commercial and residential use. By the end of 1967, there were 503 factories completed and in operation, employing more than 12% of the Colony's industrial workers. By the end of 1970, nearly all industrial sites in Kwun Tong had been developed. At Cheung Sha Wan, on the north-western part of the harbour, the seawall was extended from Sham Shui Po to complete a regular waterfront. Half of Hung Hom Bay has been filled in to provide 102 acres of land, the larger part of which forming the site of a new railway terminal and access roads to the cross-harbour road tunnel. As reclamation work progressed, it was realized that this piece of land, when formed, would be entirely cut off from the business and administration centre of Kowloon, which lay to the west of the railway line. The only access to the area east of the railway was by a single road which took traffic across the railway near the northern end of the reclamation. Until the problem of road access had been solved, the Hung Hom Bay Reclamation could be used only for temporary structures.

The years 1960 and 1961 saw the launching of large-scale development projects within and beyond the harbour limits. The Central Area Development Plan for the city of Victoria, announced in August 1961, provided for a two-level city. Provision was made in Stage III of the Plan for the berthing of river steamers. A camber was built into the harbour from the Central District to afford access to and shelter for small craft serving the port. This is an important addition to the port's amenities, since during stormy weather it is often necessary for these service craft to continue working up to the last possible moment before making a dash for shelter in a typhoon anchorage.

Also announced in 1961 was the large-scale reclamation off Wan Chai which, in 1972, is nearing completion. Besides taking up ninety acres of water space in the heart of the harbour, this scheme reduces the width of the harbour at its central constriction by almost a quarter (Fig. 17). The probable disturbance to tidal flows resulting from this and other projects that involve a change in the shape of the harbour has been a subject of great concern to all connected with port operations. Government recognition of the need to conserve water space within the harbour is reflected in recent efforts to open up areas for urban development along the Kowloon foothills, at, for example, Shek Kip Mei, Tai Wo Ping, Lo Fu Ngam, Kowloon Tsai, Tsz Wan Shan and Sau Mau Ping. As has been the experience in urban expansion on Hong Kong Island, the city in Kowloon is climbing up the hills. A beginning was made by the opening in June 1961, of a high-level road—Lung Cheung Road—that runs across the lower slopes of the Kowloon foothills, forming a major east-west route. This road, together with its extensions in Ching Cheung Road, provide much-needed access to the relatively hilly areas which are now in varying stages of development.

Shipping and Port Facilities

By far the greater part of the cargoes imported to and exported from Hong Kong is carried by ship. The Kowloon-Canton railway handled about 0·8 million tons of freight in 1970,[8] as compared with 12·8 million tons carried by ships. Except for imports of small quantities of foodstuffs, there is no road traffic between Hong Kong and China.[9] Shipping engaged in foreign trade can be divided into three types: junk traffic, near-seas shipping and ocean shipping. A clear delimitation of the area served by junks is not possible owing to the lack of organization and control in junk traffic. There is little doubt, however, that the distance that can be travelled by junks limits their sphere of activity to the South China coast and mainly to the immediate neighbourhood of Hong Kong and Macao. On the other hand, the nature of the near-seas and ocean shipping is fairly well defined. A study in 1960 by Boxer,[10] based on data from the Marine Department Shipping Reports, points out the strong correlation between type of vessels, nature of cargo and the method of transhipment in the port. The near-seas shipping is dominated by Hong Kong-owned vessels or chartered vessels under Chinese agency representation, engaged in the import of staple and general cargoes for consumption in Hong Kong and in the export of Hong Kong products. Destinations and ports of origin for this traffic are China, Taiwan, Japan, Borneo, the Straits, Siam, Cambodia and Vietnam. The Bangkok-Saigon-Phnompenh route is most commonly used and is characterized by vessels of small tonnage carrying foodstuffs. Belonging to the same group, but distinguished by their Hong Kong-European ownership, are bigger vessels engaged in the Bay of Bengal-Calcutta route, which is particularly important in the supply of raw cotton to the textile industry. Another main route followed by these vessels is southward, to Australia and New Zealand. In the port of Hong Kong most vessels in the near-seas shipping group anchor midstream, making use of government moorings, loading and unloading with the help of lighters using ship's gear. Hong Kong is the terminal port for this type of shipping, although the European-owned vessels sometimes extend their routes to Japan.

The ocean-going shipping is characterized by large vessels owned outside Hong Kong and represented by European-type agencies for long distance trading to Europe or America. These vessels serve the needs of Hong Kong as an entrepôt and as a manufacturer. A high proportion of them are berthed alongside wharves; the discharge and loading of cargoes are done both on the wharves and by lighters. Hong Kong is just one port of call among many for this type of shipping.

In the decade between 1957 and 1967 there was a remarkable growth in the volume of shipping using the port. After the long decline that resulted from the Second World War, the volume of shipping only regained its pre-war level as late as 1957–8, but it had since increased

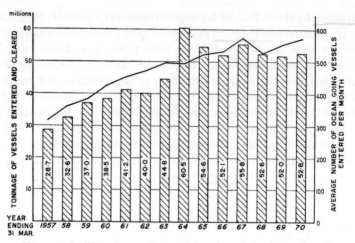

Figure 18. Tonnage and number of vessels entered and
cleared, 1957–70.

by 71% to reach 55·8 million tons in the year 1966–7 (Table 29 and
Fig. 18). The increase in the tonnage of ocean-going vessels was even
more significant: 83% in the same period. A slight decline is seen in the
total tonnage of shipping since 1967 but the volume of cargoes handled

TABLE 29. NET REGISTER TONNAGE OF VESSELS ENTERED AND CLEARED
AND CARGOES HANDLED, 1939 AND 1956–70 (IN THOUSANDS)

Year	Ocean going	River steamers	Junks and launches	Total	Cargoes handled*
1939	22,148	— 8,749 —		30,897	—
1956–7	21,982	2,291	4,440	28,713	6,579
1957–8	24,762	2,574	5,305	32,641	6,655
1960–1	32,845	2,285	6,066	41,196	7,816
1966–7	45,508	5,768**	4,559	55,835	12,439
1969–70	45,130	4,332**	3,310	52,772	12,805

* in dead weight tons.
** excluding hydrofoils.
SOURCE: Hong Kong, *Annual Report of the Director of Marine,* 1956–70.

in the year 1969–70 was the largest on record. The lack of improvement
in the tonnage of junks and launches emphasizes the role of ocean shipping. The port is becoming increasingly international; ships of thirty-
nine nations are represented in the shipping list. While British shipping

has fallen off, relatively, there has been an increase in the number of Japanese and European ships, and of ships of a number of nations new to the port. Besides those engaged in the carrying of cargoes for the port, ships have undoubtedly been drawn to the port by the efficient repair services offered by local shipyards and by the expanding popularity of Hong Kong as a tourist centre.

Despite the increasing volume of shipping using the harbour, the port of Hong Kong still provides unhampered movement and clearance. Given continued stability in Hong Kong's economic development, however, the need to provide further berthing facilities to take larger vessels likely to call at the port has to be met. At present, the greater proportion of ocean-going vessels find their berths midstream. The Government maintains seventy-one mooring-buoys in the harbour (Fig. 19) and is engaged in providing deeper water and stronger

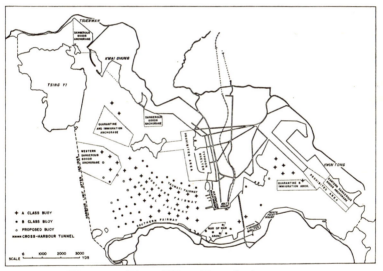

Figure 19. Plan of Hong Kong harbour, 1970.

moorings to meet the increasing demand. Among the moorings now available, forty-two are intended for vessels of up to 600 feet in length and twenty-seven for vessels of up to 450 feet. Various local interests connected with shipping have erected a further 368 private moorings in the harbour, to serve their own needs.

There are seventeen berths along wharves and quays, many of which can accommodate ships with draughts of up to thirty-six feet. All have been developed and are operated by private companies which are also engaged in lighterage, stevedoring and warehousing. The China Provident Company Ltd. and its subsidiary, North Point Wharves Ltd., operate the only commercial deep-water berths on the Island. At North Point a quay wall constructed of solid block granite provides 1,230 linear feet of berthage with thirty feet of water. The area behind the quay, developed after 1948, was designed and built for the requirements of modern shipping. Its comparatively recent development has enabled the latest type of mechanization such as mobile cranes, wall cranes, side loaders, belt-elevators and fork-lifts to be introduced. Along the full length of the quay there are transit godowns, on the rear of which are the main storage godowns, a cold storage plant and open storage. The total capacity of the covered storage and transit accommodation is 8·6 million cubic feet. Palletization, the placing of cargo on standard-size platforms, has been used for the handling and storage of small packages to simplify delivery and to reduce damage to cargoes. The company is developing a container terminal which is backed by a ten-acre freight station across the harbour in Kwun Tong.

At West Point, the China Provident Company Ltd owns extensive godown premises which have been re-built since the war into multi-storey godowns, all served by elevating machinery and internal chutes. The new cold-storage godown on the waterfront, completed in 1953, is particularly important to the near-by Western District market. Total covered storage space amounts to over 4·6 million cubic feet. Partly because the godown companies at West Point do not have the exclusive right to use the waterfront, and partly because West Point was developed originally to handle Chinese produce, mechanical aids for the movement of cargoes between the godowns and the lighters made fast to the seawall are totally lacking.

The other two wharf and godown companies, Holt's Wharf and the Hong Kong and Kowloon Wharf and Godown Company, occupy extensive areas on the south-eastern and south-western tips of the Kowloon peninsula. Holt's Wharf is operated mainly for ships of the Blue Funnel Line and the Glen Line. Although the wharf and storage facilities can also be hired by other shippers, the ships of these two companies always have first claim. There are two berths at Holt's Wharf, one of 470 feet and the other of 450 feet, each with a depth of thirty feet. Three lighter basins alongside the wharves give shelter for lighters working in rough weather. These basins are necessary since this part of the harbour is relatively exposed to the prevailing winds.

Storage space in multi-storey godowns is provided for a total of 2·7 million cubic feet. The wharves are served by steam and diesel cranes with lifting capacities of from two to five tons. No. 1 wharf at the eastern end is connected by railway to the terminus of the Kowloon-Canton railway. The use of this facility has been restricted, however, by the lifting capacity of the cranes on the wharf. Floating cranes of twenty tons capacity are therefore provided by the company. For very heavy loads, which are extremely rare in the port, ships have to be berthed at the foot of the electric cantilever (hammer head) cranes of 100–150 tons capacity at the Hong Kong and Whampoa Dock on the mainland, or at the Taikoo Dockyard on Hong Kong Island.

The Hong Kong and Kowloon Wharf and Godown Company is the largest of the companies that provide berthage for ocean-going vessels. The site developed by this Company combines the natural advantages of deep water and shelter from the prevailing winds. Along the 2,000-foot quay, transit sheds and multi-storey godowns have been built, facing four wharves which provide ten berths. These wharves are served by a road system and a light railway for the transport of goods to and from the transit sheds. Except for mobile cranes and fork-lifts, there is no mechanical equipment for loading and unloading between ship and shore. Ships berthed at these wharves have to use their own gear for cargo handling. The whole length of the quay wall is served by electric portal cranes of up to fifteen tons capacity, which are mainly employed to transfer cargoes between the godowns and lighters brought alongside the quay wall. The godowns, with a total capacity of 13·5 million cubic feet, are equipped with electric wall cranes, hoists and chutes. There is also storage for dangerous goods, timber and logs and other special cargoes.

Having the largest interest in services for ocean-going vessels, the Company has been pre-eminently concerned with the recent increase in the volume of shipping in the port and in the development of containerized and unitized cargo handling. Early in 1961, the Company began a five-year development plan which included mechanization, containerization, extension of No. 5 wharf into deeper water, and the construction of the first ocean terminal of the port. It has been realized that care for the 'human cargo' of the port has long been neglected, and the recent growth of the tourist industry has called for greater efforts to improve passenger facilities. Completed in 1966, the new terminal has a three-floor structure along a 1,250 feet long and 250 feet wide pier which can accommodate all but the very largest liners at present in use. The expansion of storage accommodation is one of the most immediate tasks in the development plan, which aims at increasing storage capacity by some 1·5 million cubic feet. Part of this expansion will be, as some has already been, sited in the new industrial towns of Tsuen Wan and Kwun Tong.

All the wharf and godown companies maintain a large fleet of lighters and towing launches for the transport of cargoes to and from vessels anchored midstream or berthed alongside wharves. The abundance of labour in the port has favoured the widespread employment of lighterage, which allows delivery on both sides of the vessel simultaneously. In addition to properly constructed steel lighters operated by the godown companies, there are many barges of all types and sizes operated by small transport companies, and a large number of Chinese junks engaged in the stevedoring business. Typical of the Chinese-owned trade or industry in Hong Kong, the junks are run as family concerns, the family crew combine a sound knowledge of seamanship and current documentary requirements for every shipment they handle. Their stevedoring services have been found to be most suitable for ships carrying general cargo for a large number of consignees. With few exceptions, junks are capable of moving under their own sail, but the past decade has seen the conversion of a large proportion of the lighters to mechanical propulsion. Movement can also be speeded up by engaging towing launches, depending on the demand of the consignee. It is not unusual for slow delivery to be preferred by cargo owners, who have difficulties in securing storage space. In most cases, the arrangement by which payments are made by the job rather than by the working hour results in considerable economy for cargo owners. As there are many junks available, there is keen competition to secure employment by making the terms of service as flexible as possible and by demanding a minimum of formalities. This had been made possible by the lack of import and export restrictions and customs regulations in the port. The total number of cargo-working craft in 1970 was about 2,150 and the changes in their composition since 1959 are shown in Figure 20.

The profitable use of Chinese-type junks and stevedoring services also owes much to the considerable length of seawall along the waterfront, which is open to the public and to all forms of land transport. The seawall, which is constructed and maintained by the Government, provides convenient landing-places at all stages of the tide. Many sections of the waterfront have been utilized as the sorting and weighing yards for small warehouses. Because of the absence of any kind of mechanical aid for the movement of cargoes on these public seawalls, many barges are equipped with their own derricks, while the masts of the Chinese junks are ingeniously fitted with a system of block and tackle to serve as slings or hoists. Such simple devices are not efficient and they are employed only when cargoes are too heavy or too bulky to be lifted by one man. Wherever possible, operations are carried out by manual labour. This method of cargo handling, inefficient though it may seem, can certainly maintain itself against mechanization as long as miscellaneous cargoes and small consignments continue to be the main concern of the port.

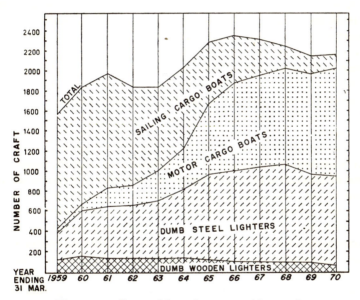

Figure 20. Composition of cargo-working craft.

Arising from the common practice of midstream anchorage, a large number of launches and motor boats are also operated in the port for specialized services, such as fuel bunkering, the supply of fresh water and provisions, and the transport of persons between ships and shore. Five oil companies established in Hong Kong have facilities for delivering oil to ships berthed alongside their installations, but most of their bunkering is carried out by special lighters which deliver oil anywhere in the harbour. The coal-bunkering service of the port is falling into disuse partly because of high costs and partly because more ships are using liquid fuel. The Hong Kong Coaling Agency, formed by three major shipping interests, has been the largest importer and supplier since government control of the distribution of coal was relinquished in 1955. Normally it has 1,000 tons in stock and the coal comes mainly from Fushun, in North-East China. For the supply of fresh water to ships berthed in the harbour, a fleet of nine motor launches is employed. Five of these specially-constructed boats belong to the Union Waterboat Company which can deliver up to 3,000 tons of water per day. The other four vessels, of 120 tons and 320 tons capacity, belong to the Leung Tai Kee Waterboat Company Ltd.

In terms of the number of ships and craft serving external trade, the port of Hong Kong already has a very high density of traffic. This is augmented by eighty-two cross-harbour passenger and vehicular ferries, which provide an indispensable link between the two parts of the city, and between the city and other districts of the New Territories. The density of this traffic is expected to increase with the growth of ferry services to provide transport to the new satellite towns now spreading east and west of Kowloon.

The administration of the port is in the hands of the Marine Department, which is responsible for the enforcement of legislation and general policy regarding shipping, and the maintenance of port efficiency. The control and operation of port facilities such as wharves, transit sheds and warehouses are, however, all in the hands of private companies. Two committees advise the Government on port administration: the Port Committee is concerned with long-term planning and construction projects contemplated by private enterprise; the Port Executive Committee, representing shipping and godown interests, deals with day-to-day problems.

Four other government departments are directly concerned in the control and management of the port. The Port Works Office, a branch of the Public Works Department, is responsible for the construction and maintenance of all port facilities which do not fall within the function of a private company to provide. This work includes the building and maintenance of seawalls, breakwaters, public piers and landing-places, moorings and lights, dredging, underwater inspection, site investigation, and such research duties as tidal current readings and the mapping of the harbour floor. The Port Health Service of the Medical Department, the Preventive Service of the Department of Industry and Commerce and the Marine Division of the Hong Kong Police are responsible for maintaining security and order in the port.

The many services and authorities which have direct influence on the movement of cargoes and passengers demonstrate the complicated problems of the operation and management of the port. The nature and size of the users of the port, which must enter into the question of the efficiency of its operation, have been described in the first part of the chapter. A discussion of the adequacy of these services, together with an exposition of the problems facing port development will be the main purpose of the concluding chapter. It is remarkable how smoothly the port functions in the hands of numerous independent operatives, a feature noted also in the observation of the Committee of Inquiry into the major ports of Great Britain, that 'there is no kind of standard pattern for the distribution of these services. The number of separate organizations depends largely on the custom of the port and the statutory powers vested in the port authority.'[11] The custom of the port of Hong Kong is characteristic of the *laissez-faire* policy and opportunism which underlie much of its success as well being the root cause of many of its deficiencies.

CHAPTER SEVEN

CONCLUSION AND PROSPECT

No comprehensive study of the growth of the Colony can fail to point out the dependence of its economy on the port. The only natural resource of Hong Kong is its magnificent harbour. At the same time, it must be recognized that there have been important human factors influencing port development. The singularity of its great natural advantage emphasizes the danger of assigning to the environmental factors a determinative influence which they do not exert.[1] From the beginning of European settlement, political forces have been particularly powerful, the port developing only after the delimitation of the political boundary that distinguished it from the rest of South China, of which it was geographically and socially a part.

Vicissitudes in the port's external relationships, especially those with China, the port's hinterland, go far to explain its economic growth. Hong Kong was a foreign creation; foreign trade determined the need for an economic base at tide water and the considerations of defence brought out the advantages of Hong Kong Island as a site. However, defensive sites have proved 'often ill-suited for urban development beyond a stage which is soon reached',[2] and land reclamation, a process that has characterized every stage of the port's development, started in the second decade of growth. Even then, the physical expansion of the city could not be achieved without changing the political boundary. The orderly functioning of the port had to await the removal of the tariff barrier dividing the harbour.

With the gift of the favourable water site, the development of port facilities was relatively easy and the cost of port operation low. The reverse was true of the development on land and of the cost of urban functions. The severity of the land problem has varied with economic and social changes, but, in general, it has been aggravated with the passage of time. The lack of room for urban expansion has been felt in most cities. In few cases, however, is the limit to urban sprawl as clearly drawn as in Hong Kong, where the mountainous backbone of the Island and the fringing range of northern Kowloon dictate that the urban area can only increase at the expense of the water area. The physical severance of the two parts of the city reduces considerably social and economic intercourse between them. It has led to very special problems of duplication of urban services as well as necessitating the maintenance of easy water access from one side of the harbour to the other.

If cross-harbour traffic continues to increase in proportion to the growth in population, congestion in the harbour could worsen. The need to remove some of the lines of internal communication from the harbour may have to be reckoned with. The matter has been given some urgency by the expected further concentration of commercial and civic activities on the Island as a result of the re-development of Central Victoria to incorporate ex-military land.[3] The provision of a cross-harbour road link became inevitable if the port was to be spared the task of choosing between restricted access to the town centre and impeded port functions. In September 1969, the construction of a four-lane cross-harbour tunnel was started and opened to traffic in August 1972. With an ultimate capacity of 72,000 vehicles per day, it is expected to remove some of the urban traffic on water. Unrestrained car ownership will, however, generate an increasing demand for cross-harbour vehicular traffic and it is envisaged[4] that additional vehicular ferry routes will have to be provided within the next decade. Some relief for congestion in the harbour may also be achieved by providing berths at piers instead of at moorings midstream. This can be effected only if access roads to the piers are adequate to make road transport competitive. The northern side of the harbour, with direct road connections with the new industrial areas of Kwun Tong and Tsuen Wan, offers better opportunities for this development.

Until the economic ties between the port and its hinterland were loosened in the past two decades, there could be no doubt that all far-reaching influences came from that direction. Trade was the life-blood of the port but the movement of people with their resources into Hong Kong was the greatest stimulus to economic and social advancement. So long as the factors affecting the movement of people were primarily economic, a balance of population could usually be adjusted to the relative prosperity of the port and its hinterland. Any marked improvement in the living conditions of Hong Kong attracted an increased inflow of surplus population from South China, a movement which in itself discouraged further inflow by lowering the average conditions of living. A large number went back as soon as circumstances would allow but sufficient always remained to inflate the population figures. Town planners had pointed out that 'if on the analogy of the Greater London Plan, new towns were to be built on the limited suitable land of Kowloon or on the much less limited land of the New Territories, they would at once be filled up from this unplumbed reservoir on the mainland'.[5] Before the Pacific War, it was the policy of the Hong Kong Government to allow Chinese freedom of movement across the border. The relationship between Hong Kong and China was so intimate that, even when it was deemed desirable, neither Government, acting singly or jointly, succeeded in stopping the movement.

One of the unique features of the development of the port, therefore, was that the growth of its population often preceded its economic progress. That the port has prospered after absorbing successive waves of immigrants says much for the resilience and adaptability of the community.

Great efforts were made by the community of the port to induce maritime interests and shippers to take advantage of its services and facilities. The free-port status was the Government's greatest contribution to this end, and there can be no doubt about the benefit conferred on the port by the maintenance of free trade in an area infested with restrictionist measures. Security and stability provided a firm foundation for economic and social improvement; private interests could then be encouraged to play the major role in developing and operating port facilities. By making full use of the abundant supply of cheap labour, economy was achieved without prejudicing efficiency. The combination of efficient warehousing, marine insurance, banking, shipping and ship-repairing, together with the situation of the port at the point of entry to China, placed Hong Kong in a very favourable position for performing entrepôt services on behalf of China and Southeast Asian countries.

The situation of the port in relation to its hinterland began to change after the Pacific War. It was the Nationalist Government of China that advocated the policy of diverting trade away from Hong Kong and the People's Government completed the disruption of the port's entrepôt function for China. The development of the commercial and shipping connections in the port was, however, too far advanced to be crippled by the loss of the hinterland and, with the resources of the last flood of immigrants, a new situation evolved in which the port incorporated the role of its hinterland and greatly expanded its foreland. The port ceased to be an important hub for coastal and inland waterway traffic. The entrepôt trade was reorientated to a much wider world-setting.

The change from an entrepôt economy to one dominated by industry emphasized the dependence of Hong Kong on the port. With no natural resources from which to draw and with the local market dominated by Chinese goods, industry has had to rely heavily on overseas markets and low transport costs. Unlike the development in most industrial ports,[6] the industries in Hong Kong are light industries of a highly-varied nature, and are primarily attracted by the abundance of cheap labour and political stability. Access to markets which offer preference is undoubtedly an additional attraction in the early stages of industrialization, but access is effected only through an efficient transport system. It is therefore imperative that the port should maintain a rapid turn-round for ships and keep its charges as light as possible.

The question of the adequacy of the port to meet present and future needs inevitably involves some consideration of the nature of Hong Kong's industries and the prospects of growth. Judging from the conditions in which industrialization took place, the weakness of Hong Kong industries is more real and more permanent than their strength. The over-concentration on textiles is evident from the figures of employment and exports. The expansion of this industry has produced complications in that manufacturers in all parts of the world, finding themselves unable to compete with Hong Kong in their domestic markets, have devised new ways and means or intensified their previous efforts to curb this invasion of cheap textiles. Industrialization in underdeveloped countries has tended to invigorate protectionist measures in the markets now open to Hong Kong products, and has absorbed a rising proportion of the raw material the Colony has been accustomed to have available. There is some evidence that the phenomenal development of Hong Kong's textile industry in the last two decades has expended its force. The removal of excessive spindles and looms from Hong Kong to foreign countries, especially to newly independent countries in Africa, is an indication of this.[7] The export of whole units of other over-expanded industries, such as enamelware, flashlight and tobacco, into these countries has already met with success, which draws further attention to this outlet for the entrepreneurial abilities of Hong Kong.

With a development strikingly similar to the rapid expansion of the textile industry, the manufacture of plastic goods grew from nothing in 1947 to take second place to textiles in Hong Kong's exports in 1960. Unorganized expansion and the glutting of markets has caused in this industry, too, a decline in its rate of growth since 1962. Although over-expanded industries continue to grow after successful attempts to develop new markets and to diversify their products, critics have looked

upon this as an indication of the lack of vision and initiative on the part
of Hong Kong industrialists. Few have given sufficient consideration,
however, to the contribution of this rough competition among local
manufacturers towards making Hong Kong products competitive in
world markets, nor have they taken sufficiently into account the need
to turn thousands of unskilled workers to the production line with
little or no overhead costs and as soon as they become available.[8]
The quest for quick profits for minimum investment, not unjustified
by the consideration of security in the Colony, militates against expenditure on investigation and experiment which must precede new lines of
production.

The most recent attempts to achieve economy and efficiency in industry are found in the joint ventures between Hong Kong and foreign
manufacturers in developing new industries which require a fair amount
of technical knowledge and skill. These operations are not expected to
lead to a marked change in either the volume or the nature of cargoes
handled by the port.

The 1961 census pointed out that in the following ten-year period,
about 800,000 new workers would expect to find employment, and the
Colony would be faced with the task of supporting an additional 90,000
to 100,000 people every year. These figures take no account of the
number of immigrants, for this cannot be estimated with any degree
of accuracy. There are good reasons to believe, however, that Hong
Kong will continue to receive waves of people from China. A continued
growth in industry and a strengthened home market with a steady rise
in overall import and export requirements may therefore be envisaged
in the port.

Although some new items have been added to the list of imports and
exports since the rise of the industrial economy, the concern of the port
is still with general cargo. This comprises a multitude of commodities
in an infinite variety of shapes and sizes which must be handled individu-
ally. The traditional method of overside break-bulk delivery to and from
lighters, using the deck winches and booms of ships in conjunction with
a maximum use of manual labour, has been found suitable for such
cargoes. Some 70% of the cargoes are still loaded or unloaded by junks
or lighters[9] and despite this primitive method of cargo handling, Hong
Kong is reputed to have the fastest turn-round time of any port in
Southeast Asia. Although it cannot be denied that the increased use of
shore machinery will reduce cargo-handling labour in the port and
increase productivity, mechanization threatens to create unemployment,

given the present social conditions. The present system of loading and unloading, however, leaves much room for improvement. Because of the general availability of the stevedoring services, local manufacturers are prone to delay the dispatch of their consignments to the ship until the last moment. Lighters and sampans usually all arrive alongside on the final day of loading, bringing goods of all descriptions for a vast number of destinations. Loading is carried out piecemeal and because of stowage arrangements in the holds of the ship, many lighters may be kept waiting by the late arrival of one consignment. Much difficulty also is experienced in sorting and unloading this mixture of consignments at destination, and this incurs higher costs.

The use of mechanical appliances on shore requires the construction of strong quays alongside which ships can be berthed. Before the coming of containerization such quays were found only at the North Point Wharves developed in the post-war period. The piers of the Hong Kong and Kowloon Wharves and Holt's Wharves, the two leading wharfingers of the port, were little more than landing-places, and had not been constructed to support heavy machinery. Again, the advantage of using shore cranes is restricted unless piers are wide enough to be equipped with railway tracks, roads, or transit sheds with quay aprons. In the port of Hong Kong nothing short of a revolutionary port-works scheme will make this possible. Some lead is provided by the ocean terminal constructed at the southern tip of Kowloon, but the primary function of this structure is to serve passengers.

The use of small mobile equipment to speed up horizontal movement across a floor or a quay and for stacking inside a warehouse has been limited to the premises of private warehouse and wharf companies. Outside these private premises, cargo-working areas are open to the public, accessible to pedestrians and to all types of land vehicles that may or may not be engaged in cargo working. The movement of cargo between ship and warehouse often has to cut across urban traffic. No specialized mechanical aid to cargo movement can be used effectively under such circumstances. The function of the waterfront is the result of a continuation of patterns of use from the early coastal and inland waterway trade carried by junks and launches. These patterns have remained standard practice and the use of mechanical cargo-handling equipment has thus been made virtually impossible over long stretches of the waterfront as at Kennedy Town, West Point, Wan Chai, Shau Kei Wan on the Island, and Sham Shui Po, Mong Kok, Yau Ma Tei and Tai Kok Tsui in Kowloon. These public cargo-working areas are scenes of acute congestion and confusion where lorries and hand-carts, junks, sampans, launches and lighters vie for parking, manoeuvring or working space. It is only since 1966 that the Government has set up a special working party to study the state of cargo working in the port with particular regard to the provision and control of cargo-working basins and the regulation of land vehicles. This government body has recommended imposing a charge for the use of improved amenities in cargo-working basins and installing a metered system for cargo-working lorries. This amounts to the collection of landing charges, the effects of which are still to be tested. On the one hand, collection of charges may help to speed up loading and unloading since lighter or lorry operators will be encouraged to vacate the cargo-working areas; on the other hand, it may produce further congestion at those sections of the waterfront where a charge collecting system has not yet been instituted.

A high standard of mechanization can be achieved only where the whole operation of cargo handling is performed by one authority. 'The greater the number of different bodies involved in port operation, the greater the premium to be placed on liaison and co-operation'.[10] Up to the present, the numerous individual operatives in the port of Hong Kong, especially in the stevedoring and the warehousing trades, have succeeded in maintaining efficiency and low cost by competition. The consideration of productivity carries little weight in present social conditions. The lack of organization, except in the few wharf and godown companies, may be tolerable as long as competition does not arise between Hong Kong and other ports in southeast China and as long as small consignments of miscellaneous cargoes predominate. While a change in the competitive power of Chinese ports may be expected in the less immediate future, in Hong Kong the proportion of large industrial units to the family type of workshops is increasing, and concentration in industrial satellite towns is an established trend. Considerable advantage may be gained by combining individual operatives under a small number of authorities to provide specialized services to these industrial nuclei, in co-operation instead of in competition. The growth over the past few years of the door-to-door concept in goods transport all over the world may provide the lead towards unified control over the whole transport chain by fewer, separate organizations.

Hong Kong has not been slow to awaken to the great revolution in construction of port works and in port operation generated by the world movement towards unitization of cargo. Shippers are already making intensive use of palletized cargo, which is specially common on the U.S. run. Units of less than two-ton weight (2,032 kilos) and less than forty cubic feet (1,133 cu.m.) are being recommended by godown and shipping companies to shippers. In 1966, both Government and private institutions began studying the possibilities of container development in Hong Kong.[11] It was widely accepted that containerization was inevitable if the port of Hong Kong was to maintain its reputation as an efficient and economic centre for cargo handling and to retain its position as a major port of call in the Far East. It is only since about 1968 that containerization has received wide attention in this area but the response has been unexpectedly vigorous. Besides actively preparing its container port for commission by late 1969, Singapore started planning a container feeder-service between itself and five ports in Malaysia[12] and Japan began building several container ports. Container shipments between the west coast of the United States and Japan are already well advanced while a start has been made on a container service between Europe, Australia and Japan. A new port hierarchy is evolving in which a few main focal ports operating on an intensive scale relegate other ports to feeder status.[13] The position of Hong Kong in the new hierarchy depends largely on its own containerization programme.

However, containerization in Hong Kong faces special problems. Because of the predominance of general cargo and small consignments in the import and export trades, and because of the lack of stacking or storage room in most factories, Hong Kong goods will have to be packed and unpacked at the container terminal depot and moved inland by conventional means. This eliminates the ideal 'door-to-door flow line system' and reduces the savings in stevedoring cost; besides, 'the more heterogeneous the cargo consignments and the more numerous their destinations, the greater is the organizational problem.'[14] The highly unbalanced volumes of Hong Kong's import and export trades also present problems in maintaining a parallel export-import flow of fully-loaded containers. Nevertheless, the port will still benefit from the reduced turn-round time of ships[15] and the quicker transit period for some traffic. The export in containers of a variety of Hong Kong products, such as cameras, clocks and textiles, has for some time enjoyed more favourable overall rates. Clothing and garments, which are the leading items of export by value, have benefited from the 'hangtainers', built by the Hong Kong and Kowloon Wharf and Godown Company, which provide wardrobe packing and make cleaning and pressing before retail sale unnecessary.

An inquiry directed by the Government in 1966 resulted in recommendations for a $261 million and 115 acre project[16] to provide for a four-berth container terminal at Kwai Chung (Fig. 21), to be completed

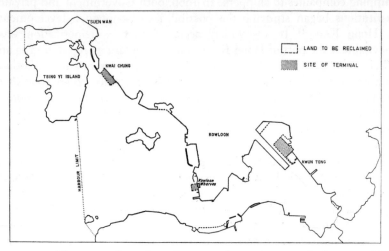

Figure 21. Location of proposed container terminals.

in stages within six years. As in all previous attempts at improving port facilities, the Government is only one of the interested parties in the development of this terminal; private enterprise was encouraged to come forward with its own proposals. Following the publication of the Container Committee's report on the Kwai Chung project, the Hong Kong and Kowloon Wharf and Godown Company announced, in mid-1967, another plan for a three-berth container terminal to be constructed at the northern end of their premises at Tsim Sha Tsui (Fig. 22). Early in 1969, the North Point Wharves, a subsidiary of the China Provident Company, also proposed to develop a containership berth at North Point, with a marshalling yard and back-up facilities at Ngau Tau Kok on the other side of the harbour, the physical link to be provided by a cargo-ferry service. The Kowloon Wharf and Godown Company decided to redevelop part of its existing property, including the addition by reclamation of twenty-nine acres. Because of the economies gained by adapting existing equipment and facilities, the cost of this project was estimated at only $70 million. The management of the Company (with experience of handling 400 containers a month in 1966 and up to 800 a month in 1968) initially considered the expensive

Kwai Chung project unwarranted, at least until more firm guidance was given by shipping companies concerning the planned number and frequency of container-shipping services to Hong Kong.[17]

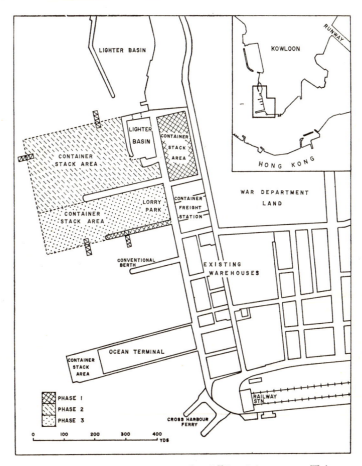

Figure 22. Planned container berth development at Tsim Sha Tsui.

A comparison of the three proposed schemes shows that the Tsim Sha Tsui site has the advantage of a central position in the harbour with ready access to existing warehouses where indoor sorting and packing facilities and covered loading-space are already provided. The North Point site, though further away from the centre and relatively more exposed, enjoys the same advantage of ready access to existing ware-houses. There is also the vast range of back-up facilities for cargo movement such as mobile cranes, trailers, forklifts and pallets. The Kwai Chung site needs completely new facilities. The central position of the Tsim Sha Tsui site is important because the physical layout of the port and the type of cargo it handles call for the frequent use of lighters that concentrate in the two typhoon shelters of Mong Kok and Causeway Bay. Lighter trips to and from the Tsim Sha Tsui site are relatively short. On the other hand, the lack of space for expansion at this site is a very serious drawback. The same applies to the North Point site. Because of the need to look ahead to further expansion, in those European and American ports where containerization is well advanced, the sites chosen for development are new locations outside main cities. This same calculation adds much to the attraction of the Kwai Chung site, where further reclamation would be far more tolerable than at Tsim Sha Tsui or at North Point. Moreover, container berth development at Tsim Sha Tsui would lead to a further concentration of port activities at an already congested part of the port, while development at Kwai Chung would lead to some degree of decentralization.

All three sites are detached from the railway line, and, as far as can be reasoned, there is no possibility of effecting a railway link to these sites even should the need arise. It seems that planners, in putting forward the schemes, have not considered the railway as one of the links in the chain of through transport. While it would be difficult, judging from the political and economic development of the last two decades, to envisage streams of containers running on unit trains in and out of China in the near future, a study of the history of port development in Hong Kong makes it even more difficult to conclude that the railway will not be of service to a container port in this part of the world. However, the report of the Container Committee did provide the basis for a serious rethinking of the port's immediate future and the Committee has remained in existence in order to advise the Government on container service development.

Reflecting the strong upsurge in world-wide interest in container shipping and the conviction of the inevitability of containerization in Hong Kong, development work was started in all three sites within the period 1970–1. Conversion work was also undertaken by the two dock companies to serve container vessels. As early as 1968, the Hong Kong and Kowloon Wharf and Godown Company decided to go ahead with its Tsim Sha Tsui scheme while recommending to Government that in the long term, the Kwai Chung scheme should be implemented. As a result of the forward-looking policy of the company, the first container gantry crane of the port started to operate on No. 5 pier of the company in May 1971. North Point Wharves also developed its container terminal on the island, which was backed by a ten-acre freight depot across the harbour in Kwun Tong. In Kwai Chung, the first container berth owned by Modern Terminals Ltd., a private company, was opened to service the first container ship in September 1972. The second berth is expected to be operational in January 1973 and the third in mid-1973.

To enable the large container ships to reach berth at Kwai Chung, the Government has dredged more than three million cubic yards of seabed material from the Rambler Channel to provide a channel of 40 feet below chart datum which was the minimum depth required for large container ships. One and a half miles of access road to the terminal is being built to link up with the trunk road system, in which considerable improvement is expected when the Kowloon Foothill Road corridor is completed in 1975.

The move towards containerization presents a major challenge to the port's traditional buoy-lighter-lorry chain of cargo handling. Besides the large-scale readjustment and modification in equipment and physical layout, tremendous social problems are expected to arise from labour redundancy, retraining and re-employment. At present, palletization alone enables a workgang to load fifty to sixty tons an hour instead of the former average of fifteen tons. When full containerization is developed the loading total per gang-hour is expected to reach 150 tons. These figures provide some indication of the degree of labour redundancy that may occur, although complete containerization of cargoes in Hong Kong is unlikely ever to happen. Steel lighters have already been built for the large wharf and godown companies, which will be able to dispatch eight containers at a time to and from container ships. Many Chinese lightermen will have to follow this lead if they want to stay in business. Alternatively, they will have to stick to the conventional practice of break-bulk handling and deliver cargo to and from warehouses and container depots.

The probable growth of Hong Kong's industry and population leads to the conclusion that port capacity will have to be increased. On the other hand, the coming of containerization requires the rethinking of the nature of any new port facilities and of the future of break-bulk cargo handling. Since the design and structure of port works and the character and composition of merchant fleets are being revolutionized, it is doubtful if further provisions for the traditional system of cargo working will be justified.[18]

Planning of port development in Hong Kong has been made difficult by the impracticability of forecasting foreign trade, since this is so overwhelmingly dependent on political factors. It has been demonstrated clearly in the evolution of the present port that external influences can have no precedent and that ways and means of meeting them have to be devised as and when they arise. The rapidity with which economic and social conditions have been changing, and the nature of the foreign policy of the government of China, more than justify a cautious attitude on the part of private investors. Much uncertainty still hangs over the political future of the Colony. In a study of the urban geography of Hong Kong, Hughes (1951) pointed out that the expiry of the lease of the New Territories in 1997 'already enters into the calculations of property owners in the Colony and after 1970 may be expected to have a marked effect on development beyond Boundary Street'[19] the line that separates the leased from the ceded territories. In the light of the development that has been effected since 1951, however, the distinction between the northern and southern parts of Boundary Street is unrealistic. Any change in the political status of the New Territories will affect the entire Colony.

In the absence of long-term planning, port development tends to follow the line of least resistance, with the selection of the cheapest or the most expedient solution in each individual case. There exists a fundamental need for closer government supervision to ensure that a *laissez-faire* attitude towards port development does not allow it to degenerate into chaos.

NOTES

CHAPTER I   THE PHYSICAL SETTING (pp. 1–12)

[1] All historical studies of the birth of the Colony of Hong Kong have references to the pirates in and around the harbour. Special emphasis is given by Fox, G., *British Admirals and Chinese Pirates*, 1940.

[2] Davis, S. G., *Hong Kong in its Geographical Setting*, 1949, p. 33.

[3] Berry, L. and Ruxton, B. P., 'Weathering of Granite and Associated Erosional Features in Hong Kong', *Bulletin of Geological Society of America*, 68, 1957, 1263–92.

[4] Berry, L., 'Superficial Deposits of the Hong Kong Harbour Area', *Hong Kong University Engineering Journal*, XXI, 1957, 38–50.

[5] Davis, S. G. and Tregear, M., 'Man Kok Tsui, Lantau Island, Hong Kong', *Asian Perspectives*, 14, 1960, 183–212, and Davis, S. G., 'Archaeological Discovery in and around Hong Kong', *Journal of the Hong Kong Branch of the Royal Asiatic Society*, 5, 1965, 9–19.

[6] Morgan, F. W., *Ports and Harbours*, 1958, p. 41.

[7] Davis, S. G., *Hong Kong*, 1949, p. 119.

[8] Hong Kong Royal Observatory, *The Effect of Meteorological Conditions on Tide Height at Hong Kong*, by I. E. M. Watts, 1959.

[9] *ibid.*, p. 28.

[10] Hulse, C., *The Local Master's Handbook*, 1960.

[11] Hong Kong Royal Observatory, *Hong Kong Typhoons*, by G. S. P. Heywood, 1950.

[12] Hong Kong Royal Observatory, *Annual Departmental Report by the Director 1960–1*, 1961.

[13] Watts, I. E. M., *Meteorological Conditions*, 1959.

[14] Hong Kong Royal Observatory, *Surface Pressure Patterns and Weather Around the Year in Hong Kong*, by G. S. P. Heywood, 1953.

[15] Hong Kong Royal Observatory, *Fogs at Waglan Island and Their Relationship to Fogs in Hong Kong Harbour*, by K. R. Hung, 1951.

[16] *ibid.*, p. 12.

CHAPTER 2   FOUNDATIONS OF THE ENTREPÔT TRADE (pp. 13–33)

[1] Colonial Office, Dispatch from Lord Derby to Sir Henry Pottinger, No. 8, 3 June 1843.

[2] Morse, H. B., *The Chronicles of the East India Company Trading to China, 1635–1843*, 1929, Vol. IV, p. 2.

[3] The basic coin in foreign commerce at Canton during this period was the Spanish dollar, with an intrinsic value of 4s. 2d. and an exchange value ranging from 3s. 11d. to 5s. Greenberg, M., *British Trade and the Opening of China 1800–42*, 1951, p. vii and p. 139.

[4] Morse, H. B., *Chronicles;* Bernard, W. D., *Narrative of the Voyages and Services of the Nemesis from 1840 to 1843*, 1844; Eitel, E. J., *Europe in China*, 1895.

[5] Black, W. T., 'Sanitary State of Hong Kong in 1865', *The Edinburgh Medical Journal*, Dec. 1869.

[6] Allen, G. C. and Donnithorne, A. G., *Western Enterprise in Far Eastern Economic Development*, 1954, p. 155.

[7] Roxby, B. M. (ed.), *China Proper*, Geographical Handbook Series, 1944, Vol. I, Chapter 6, and Vol. IV, p. 254–7.

[8] Gull, E. M., *British Economic Interests in the Far East*, 1943, p. 19–20.

[9] Endacott, G. B., *A History of Hong Kong*, 1958, p. 10.

[10] Eitel, E. J., *Europe in China*, p. 112.

[11] *ibid.*, p. 60.

[12] Foreign Office, Dispatch from Lord Palmerston to Elliot, No. 1, 21 April 1841.

[13] Braga, J. M. (ed.), *Hong Kong Business Symposium*, 1957, p. 277.

[14] Bernard, W. D., *Nemesis*, p. 87.

[15] Hong Kong Government, *Report on the Blue Book*, 1854.

[16] Hong Kong Government, *Report on the Blue Book*, 1855.

[17] Berry, L. and Ruxton, B. P., 'The Evolution of Hong Kong Harbour Basin', *Annals of Geomorphology*, vol. 4, fasc. 2, 1960, p. 97–115.

[18] Although occupied in January 1841, Hong Kong was declared a British Colony on 26 June 1843. The Secretary of State informed Pottinger (Foreign Office, Dispatch No. 4, 31 January 1842) that the Island should be considered a mere military position, and that all building not required in that light should be discontinued.

[19] Endacott, G. B., *History*, p. 210–12.

[20] Hong Kong Government, *Report on the Blue Book*, 1889.

[21] The Hong Kong Government collection of paintings in the Museum and Art Gallery, City Hall, Hong Kong.

[22] The races of the tea clippers in the 1860s did not affect Hong Kong. They were run mainly between Foochow or Shanghai and England.

[23] Lamont Dock and Hope Dock at Aberdeen, Cosmopolitan Dock at Tai Kok Tsui and the Union Docks at Hunghom.

[24] *Hong Kong Telegraph*, Commercial and Statistical Papers, No. 1, April 1897.

[25] Owen, Sir David, *Future Control and Development of the Port of Hong Kong*, 1941.

[26] Sargent, A. J., *Anglo-Chinese Commerce and Diplomacy*, 1907, p. 106.

[27] *Further Statements and Suggestions regarding Hong Kong addressed to the Hon. Francis Cott, M.P.,* London, 1851.

[28] Macao was declared an open port in 1845 by the Portuguese in an attempt to regain some of the trade it had lost to Hong Kong.

[29] Lorchas were vessels with foreign-type hulls and Chinese sails, averaging about 60 tons, nearly all of which were owned and manned by Chinese.

[30] Hong Kong Government, *Annual Blue Book of Statistics,* 1845 and 1850.

[31] Hong Kong Government, *Report on the Blue Book,* 1853.

[32] Pennell, W. V., *History of the Hong Kong General Chamber of Commerce, 1861–1961,* 1961, p. 2.

[33] Banister, T. R., *A History of the External Trade of China, 1834–1881,* 1932.

[34] Colonial Office, Sir William Des Voeux to Lord Knutsford, *Colonial Possessions* Paper No. 84, 31 October 1889.

CHAPTER 3   DEVELOPMENT PRIOR TO THE SECOND WORLD WAR (pp. 34–63)

[1] Banister, T. R., *External Trade;* Hong Kong Government, *Report on the Blue Book,* 1900.

[2] Sailing ships still visited the port of Hong Kong after 1900; there were 42 in 1920, 26 of which were British and 9 American.

[3] Hong Kong, *Sessional Papers,* 1902, and 1903.

[4] Hong Kong, *Report of the Inter-Departmental Working Party on the Proposed Cross-Harbour Tunnel,* 1956.

[5] Tregear, T. R. and Berry, L., *The Development of Hong Kong and Kowloon as Told in Maps,* 1959.

[6] 'Praya East Reclamation Scheme Final Report', Hong Kong, *Sessional Papers,* 1931.

[7] Tregear, T. R. and Berry, L., *Development of Hong Kong,* p. 11.

[8] Hong Kong, *Sessional Papers,* 1901 and 1931.

[9] Hong Kong, *Sessional Papers,* 1903.

[10] Hong Kong, *Sessional Papers,* 1904.

[11] Hong Kong, *Sessional Papers,* 1903.

[12] Hong Kong Census Report, *Sessional Papers,* 1901; *Joint Consulting Engineers' Report on a Proposed Road Crossing of Hong Kong Harbour,* 1961.

[13] Hong Kong, *Sessional Papers,* 1903.

[14] Hong Kong General Chamber of Commerce, *Report of the Committee,* 1908.

[15] These figures include only those officially recorded in the typhoons of 9 November 1900; 18 September 1906; and 27 July 1908.

[16] All but 11 of the 74 gales recorded in the periods 1884–1941 and 1946–7 set in from the north-east quadrant. Hong Kong Royal Observatory, *Hong Kong Typhoons.*

[17] Hong Kong, Port Development Department, *Report of the Commercial Development of the Port of Hong Kong,* by John Duncan, 1924.

[18] Messrs Coode, Fitzmaurice, Wilson and Mitchell, Consulting Engineers to the Crown Agent, Report dated 24 November 1922.

[19] Owen, Sir David, *Future Control and Development.*

[20] *ibid.,* p. 13.

[21] *ibid.,* pp. 9 and 21.

[22] *ibid.,* p. 6.

[23] Braga, J. M., *Business Symposium,* p. 185.

[24] Hong Kong Government, *Annual Report,* 1913.

[25] Hong Kong Government, *Annual Report,* 1938.

[26] Hambro, Edward, *The Problem of Chinese Refugees in Hong Kong,* 1955.

[27] Chang, Kia-Ngau, *China's Struggle for Railroad Development,* 1943.

[28] Hong Kong General Chamber of Commerce, *Report of the Committee,* 1905, 1906 and 1908.

[29] Chang, Kia-Ngau, *Railroad development,* p. 185.

[30] Remer, C. F., *A Study of Chinese Boycotts,* 1933.

[31] *ibid.,* p. 103.

[32] Hong Kong General Chamber of Commerce, *Report of the Committee,* 1925.

[33] Hong Kong, *Historical and Statistical Abstract of the Colony of Hong Kong 1841–1930,* 1932.

[34] Hong Kong, *Report of the Economic Commission appointed to inquire into the causes and effects of the present trade depression in Hong Kong and make recommendations for the amelioration of the existing position, and for the improvement of the trade of the Colony, July 1934–February 1935,* 1935.

[35] Hong Kong Government, *Annual Report,* 1938; *The Hong Kong Exporter and Far East Importer,* 1958–9.

CHAPTER 4   DESTRUCTION AND REHABILITATION, 1941–46 (pp. 64–75)

[1] Keeton, G. W., *China, the Far East and the Future,* 1943; Mills, L. A., *British Rule in Eastern Asia,* 1942; Emerson, R., Mills, L. A. and Thompson, V., *Government and Nationalism in South East Asia,* 1942.

[2] Kirby, S. W., *The War Against Japan,* 1957, Vol. I, p. 2.

[3] Major-General C. M. Maltby's dispatch, 'Operation in Hong Kong from 8 to 25 December, 1941', *Supplement to London Gazette,* 27 January 1948; *A Record of the Actions of the Hong Kong Volunteer Defence Corps in the Battle for Hong Kong, December 1941.*

[4] Marsman, J. H., *I Escaped from Hong Kong,* 1942.

[5] Cheng, Yu-kwei, *Foreign Trade and Industrial Development of China,* 1956.

[6] Hinton, W. J., 'Hong Kong's Place in the British Empire', *Journal of the Royal Central Asian Society,* 28, 1941; Keeton, G. W., *China the Far East and the Future.*

[7] Endacott, G. B., *History.*

[8] Pennell, W. V., *Chamber of Commerce,* p. 67.

[9] Estimates made by the British Military Administration, April 1946.

[10] Hong Kong, *Final Report of the Building Reconstruction Advisory Committee,* 1946.

[11] Great Britain, Board of Trade, *Report of the United Kingdom Trade Mission to China, October to December 1946,* London, 1948.

[12] United Nations Relief and Rehabilitation Administration.

[13] Pennell, W. V., *Chamber of Commerce,* p. 69.

[14] *The Economist,* 17 August 1946, p. 260.

CHAPTER 5   RECONSTRUCTION AND INDUSTRIALIZATION, 1946–50 (pp. 76–98)

[1] Davis, S. G., *Hong Kong in its Geographical Setting,* 1949; Endacott, G. B., *History,* 1958; Szczepanik, E., *The Economic Growth of Hong Kong,* 1958.

[2] *The Economist,* 17 August 1946, p. 260; Hong Kong Government, *Annual Report,* 1946.

[3] Great Britain, Board of Trade, *Report of the United Kingdom Trade Mission to China, October to December, 1946,* London, 1948, p. 36.

[4] With retail prices in March 1939 as base, the index for 1947–9 has been found to fluctuate between 503 and 653. Hong Kong, Department of Statistics, *Report on Post-war Movements in the Cost of Living in Hong Kong,* 1950.

[5] The year 1947–8 has been regarded as the first year of post-war stabilization in the Colony. Ma, Ronald A., and Szczepanik, E., *The National Income of Hong Kong 1947–50,* 1955, p. 3.

[6] Exports of cotton products from China were valued at US$1,368,000 in 1946, rising to US$45,557,000 in 1947 and US$65,712,000 in 1948. Cheng, Yu-kwei, *Foreign Trade and Industrial Development of China.*

[7] Hong Kong, Marine Department, *Annual Report by the Director,* 1950–1; Hong Kong General Chamber of Commerce, *Report of the Committee,* 1949.

[8] Szczepanik, E., *Economic growth,* p. 47.

[9] Estimate made by the Chairman of the Hong Kong Stock Exchange, *Far Eastern Economic Review,* IX, no. 2, 1950.

[10] *Far Eastern Economic Review,* VIII, no. 26, 1950.

[11] Hong Kong, Colonial Secretariat, *Papers on Development of Kai Tak Airport,* 1954.

[12] Abercrombie, Sir Patrick, *Hong Kong Preliminary Planning Report,* 1948, p. 9.

[13] *ibid.,* p. 4.

[14] People attracted to Hong Kong by the opportunities of trade and industry it offered and for other economic reasons, as distinct from the 1949 influx which was spurred by the Communist victories; most of the latter group were political refugees. Although no correlation has been proved to exist between the motive and the time of immigration, a United Nations survey in 1954 gave support to the broad division made by the Hong Kong Government of 'economic immigrants' before 1949 and political refugees after. Hambro, E., *Chinese Refugees* and Hong Kong Government, *A Problem of People,* 1956.

[15] Hong Kong Government, *Annual Report,* 1957.

[16] Hong Kong Government, *Annual Report,* 1958, p. 132; Dwyer, D. J., 'The Problem of In-Migration and Squatter Settlement in Asian Cities: Two Case Studies, Manila and Victoria-Kowloon', *Asian Studies,* 2, No. 2, 1964, p. 145–69.

[17] Morgan, F. W., *Ports and Harbours,* 1958, p. 132.

[18] Great Britain, Board of Trade, *Report of the United Kingdom Trade Mission to China, October to December, 1946,* London, 1948.

[19] Fan, W. and Shepherd, A., 'Shipbreaking in Hong Kong', in *Symposium on Land Use and Mineral Deposits in Hong Kong and South China,* 1961.

[20] Hong Kong, Labour Department, Annual Report by the Commissioner, 1947–51.

CHAPTER 6   MODERNIZATION OF THE PORT (pp. 99–115)

[1] Boxer, B., *Ocean Shipping in the Evolution of Hong Kong,* 1961.

[2] Main items of these commodities were fertilizers, base metals, chemical elements and compounds, manufactures, and animal and vegetable crude material. Szczepanik, E., *Economic Growth.*

[3] Sargent, A. J., *Seaports and Hinterland,* 1938, p. 25.

[4] The 1967 figure would have been higher had it not been for the temporary disruption of trade with China resulting from the political confrontation. Hong Kong Government, *Annual Report,* 1967 and Hong Kong, Commerce and Industry Department, *Review of Overseas Trade in 1967,* 1968.

[5] *The Aeroplane,* 96, no. 2477, 1960, p. 215.

[6] Fan, W, and Shepherd, A., *op.cit.*

[7] Abercrombie, Sir Patrick, *Planning Report,* p. 17.

[8] Hong Kong Government, *Annual Report,* 1970.

[9] At Man Kam To, an average of 20 to 30 truck loads of fresh vegetables, eggs and live animals passed into Hong Kong every day in 1966–7.

[10] Boxer, B., *Ocean Shipping.*

[11] Great Britain, Ministry of Transport, *Report of the Committee of Inquiry into the Major Ports of Great Britain,* London, 1962, p. 30.

CHAPTER 7   CONCLUSION AND PROSPECT (pp. 116–28)

[1] Barrows, H. H., 'Geography as Human Ecology', *Annals of the Association of American Geographers*, 13, 1923.

[2] Smailes, A. E., *The Geography of Towns*, 1957, p. 52.

[3] Hong Kong, Town Planning Board, *City of Victoria, Hong Kong Central Area Redevelopment*, Report by the Director of Public Works, 1961.

[4] Traffic and Transport Survey Unit, Public Works Department, Hong Kong, Technical Report No. 68, *Cross Harbour Vehicle Movement by Ferry*, 1970.

[5] Abercrombie, Sir Patrick, *Planning Report*, p. 4.

[6] Morgan, F. W., *Ports and Harbours*, p. 132–3.

[7] *Far Eastern Economic Review*, XXXVI, No. 4 and XXXVIII, No. 3, 1962.

[8] The 1961 census finds no significant correlation between length of residence in the Colony and employment status. New arrivals do not find it more difficult to get permanent, monthly-paid work.

[9] *Hong Kong Enterprise*, May 1968, p. 26.

[10] Great Britain, Ministry of Transport, *Report of the Committee of Inquiry into the Major Ports of Great Britain*, London, 1962, p. 31.

[11] Hong Kong, Container Committee, *Report of the Container Committee*, 1966 and *Second Report and Recommendations*, 1967.

[12] *Far Eastern Economic Review*, LXI, No. 33, 1968, p. 325.

[13] Hilling, D., 'Report on the UN Seminar on Containerization', *The Dock and Harbour Authority*, August 1967, p. 121–4.

[14] Bird, J., *The Major Seaports of the United Kingdom*, 1963, p. 420.

[15] Turn-round time will be cut to 25% of what it is now, once full containerization operations get under way. *Hong Kong Enterprise*, May 1968, p. 26. See also Johnson, K. M. and Garnett, H. C., *The Economics of Containerization*, 1971, Chapter 3.

[16] Excluding the cost of the 95 acres of land which is to be reclaimed from shallow water.

[17] Forsgate, H. M. G., general manager of the Hong Kong and Kowloon Wharf and Godown Company, quoted in *South China Morning Post*, Hong Kong, 22 June 1967.

[18] It has been estimated that one container ship on strict schedule could replace five conventional ships spending 60% of their life in port. Where ports have been using piers and deliver cargo alongside, there will in fact be a surplus of conventional piers. Salisbury, P. R. 'Comparative Container Ship Design', *Shipping World and Shipbuilder*, June 1968, p. 951–4.

[19] Hughes, R. H., 'Hong Kong: An Urban Study', *Geographical Journal*, CXVII, 1951, p. 17.

BIBLIOGRAPHY

Abercrombie, Sir Patrick. *Hong Kong Preliminary Planning Report,* Hong Kong, 1948.

Allen, G. C. and Donnithorne, A. G. *Western Enterprise in Far Eastern Economic Development,* London, 1954.

Banister, T. R. *A History of the External Trade of China, 1834–81,* London, 1932.

Barrows, H. H. 'Geography as Human Ecology', *Annals of the Association of American Geographers,* Vol. 13, 1923.

Bernard, W. D. *Narrative of the Voyages and Services of the Nemesis from 1840 to 1843,* London, 1944.

Berry, L. 'Superficial Deposits of the Hong Kong Harbour Area', *Hong Kong University Engineering Journal,* XXI, 1957, 38–50.

Berry, L. and Ruxton, B. P. 'Weathering of Granite and Associated Erosional Features in Hong Kong', *Bulletin of Geological Society of America,* 68, 1957, 1263–92.

Berry, L. and Ruxton, B. P. 'The Evolution of Hong Kong Harbour Basin', *Annals of Geomorphology,* 4, 1960, 97–115.

Bird, J. *The Major Seaports of the United Kingdom,* London, 1963.

Bird, J. *Seaports and Seaport Terminals,* London, 1971.

Black, W. T. 'Sanitary State of Hong Kong in 1864', *The Edinburgh Medical Journal,* December 1869.

Boxer, B. *Ocean Shipping in the Evolution of Hong Kong,* Chicago, 1961.

Braga, J. M. *Hong Kong Business Symposium,* Hong Kong, 1957.

Chang, Kia-Ngau. *China's Struggle for Railroad Development,* New York, 1943.

Cheng, Yu-kwei. *Foreign Trade and Industrial Development of China,* Washington, 1956.

Collins, Sir Charles. *Public Administration in Hong Kong,* London, 1952.

Davis, S. G. *Hong Kong in its Geographical Setting,* London, 1949.

Davis, S. G. 'Archaeological Discovery in and around Hong Kong', *Journal of the Hong Kong Branch of the Royal Asiatic Society,* 5, 1965, 9–19.

Davis, S. G. and Tregear, M. 'Man Kok Tsui, Lantau Island, Hong Kong', *Asian Perspectives,* 4, 1960, 183–212.

Dwyer, D. J. 'The Problem of In-Migration and Squatter Settlement in Asian Cities: two case studies, Manila and Victoria Kowloon', *Asian Studies,* 11, No. 2, 1964, 145–69.

Eitel, E. J. *Europe in China,* London, 1895.

Emerson, R., Mills, L. A. and Thompson, V. *Government and Nationalism in South East Asia,* London, 1942.

Endacott, G. B. *A History of Hong Kong*, London, 1958.

Fan, W. and Shepherd, A. 'Shipbreaking in Hong Kong', *Symposium on Land Use and Mineral Deposits in Hong Kong and South China*, S. G. Davis ed., Hong Kong, 1961.

Fox, C. *British Admirals and Chinese Pirates*, London, 1940.

Fugl-Meyer, H. *The Modern Port*, Copenhagen, 1957.

Great Britain. Board of Trade. *Report of the United Kingdom Trade Mission to China, October to December 1946*, London, H.M.S.O., 1948.

Great Britain. Ministry of Transport. *Report of the Committee of Enquiry into the Major Ports of Great Britain*, London, H.M.S.O., 1962.

Greenberg, M. *British Trade and the Opening of China 1800–42*, London, 1951.

Gull, E. M. *British Economic Interests in the Far East*, London, 1943.

Hambro, Edward. *The Problem of Chinese Refugees in Hong Kong*, Sijthoff, 1955.

Harcourt, Cecil. *The Military Administration of Hong Kong, August 1945 to April 1946*, London, 1946.

Hilling, D. 'Report on the United Nations Seminar on Containerization', *The Dock and Harbour Authority*, August 1967, p. 121–4.

Hinton, W. J. 'Hong Kong's Place in the British Empire', *Journal of the Royal Central Asian Society*, 28, 1941, 256–69.

Hong Kong. *Historical and Statistical Abstract of the Colony of Hong Kong 1841–1930*, 1932.

Hong Kong. *Building Reconstruction Advisory Committee. Final Report*, 1946.

Hong Kong. Census Department. *Hong Kong Census Reports*, 1841–1941, (irregular, publisher varies, published in Hong Kong Sessional Papers or Government Gazettes).

Hong Kong. Census Department. *Report on the 1961 Census*, by K. M. A. Barnett, 1962.

Hong Kong. Census and Statistics Department. *Report on the 1966 By-Census*, by K. M. A. Barnett, 1968.

Hong Kong. Colonial Secretariat. *Papers on Development of Kai Tak Airport*, 1954.

Hong Kong. Commerce and Industry Department. *Review of Overseas Trade in 1967*, 1968.

Hong Kong. Commerce and Industry Department, Statistical Branch. *Cost of Living Survey, 1958–63/64*, prepared for the Cost of Living Review Committee, 1965.

Hong Kong. Commission Appointed to Inquire into the causes and effects of the present Trade Depression in Hong Kong, and make Recommendations for the Amelioration of the Existing Position, and for the Improvement of the Trade of the Colony, July 1934–February 1935. *Report*, 1935.

Hong Kong. Container Committee. *Report of the Container Committee*, 1966.

Hong Kong. Container Committee. *Second Report and Recommendations,* 1967.

Hong Kong. Crown Lands and Survey Office. Colony Outline Planning Team. *Land Utilization in Hong Kong as at 31st March 1966,* 1967.

Hong Kong. Department of Statistics. *Report on Post-War Movements in the Cost of Living in Hong Kong,* 1950.

Hong Kong. Harbour Ferry Services Advisory Committee. *Report of the Harbour Ferry Services Advisory Committee,* 1951.

Hong Kong. Inter-Departmental Working Party on the Proposed Cross-Harbour Tunnel. *Report of the Inter-Departmental Working Party on the Proposed Cross-Harbour Tunnel,* 1956.

Hong Kong. Marine Department. *The Port of Hong Kong,* 1967.

Hong Kong. Passenger Transport Survey Unit. *Hong Kong Passenger Transport Survey, 1964-6.* by E. Dalby, 1967.

Hong Kong. Port Development Department. *Report on the Commercial Development of the Port of Hong Kong,* by John Duncan, 1924.

Hong Kong. Port Works Division. *Engineering Report on the Proposed Container Terminal at Kwai Chung,* 1969.

Hong Kong. Public Works Department. *Harbour Improvement Report,* by J. F. Boulton, 1904.

Hong Kong. Royal Observatory. *A Statistical Survey of Typhoons and Tropical Depressions in the Western Pacific and China Sea Area,* by L. Starbuck, 1951.

Hong Kong. Royal Observatory. *The Effect of Meteorological Conditions on Tide Heights at Hong Kong,* by I. E. M. Watts, 1959.

Hong Kong. Royal Observatory. *Fogs at Waglan Island and Their Relationship to Fogs in Hong Kong Harbour,* by K. R. Hung, 1951.

Hong Kong. Royal Observatory. *Meteorological Information for Aviation Purposes,* by P. Peterson, 1964.

Hong Kong. Royal Observatory. *Hong Kong Meteorological Records and Climatological Notes 60 Years, 1884-1939, 1947-50,* ed. by J. E. Peacock, 1952.

Hong Kong. Royal Observatory. *Hong Kong Typhoons,* by G. S. P. Heywood, 1950.

Hong Kong. Royal Observatory. *Storm Surges in Hong Kong,* by T. T. Cheng, 1967.

Hong Kong. Royal Observatory. *Surface Pressure Patterns and Weather Around the Year in Hong Kong,* by G. S. P. Heywood, 1953.

Hong Kong. Royal Observatory. *Tropical Cyclones in the Western Pacific and China Sea Area from 1884 to 1953,* by P. C. Chin, 1958.

Hong Kong. Royal Observatory. *Wave Heights in the Southeast Approaches to Hong Kong Harbour,* by M. J. Cuming, 1967.

Hong Kong. Town Planning Board. *City of Victoria, Hong Kong, Central Area Redevelopment,* Report by the Director of Public Works, 1961.

Hong Kong and Whampoa Dock Company Ltd. *A Record of Thirty-Six Years,* Hong Kong, 1902.

Hughes, R. H. 'Hong Kong: An Urban Study', *Geographical Journal,* Vol. CXVII, 1951, pp. 1–23.

Hulse, C. *Local Master's Handbook,* Hong Kong, 1960.

Ingrams, Harold. *Hong Kong,* London, H.M.S.O., 1952.

Johnson, K. M. and Garnett, H. C. *The Economics of Containerisation,* London, 1971.

Keeton, G. W. *China, the Far East and the Future,* London, 1943.

Kirby, S. W. *The War Against Japan,* London, 1957.

Lo, Hsiang-lin. *Hong Kong and its External Communications Before 1842,* (in Chinese) Hong Kong, 1959.

Ma, R. A. and Szczepanik, E. *The National Income of Hong Kong, 1947–50,* Hong Kong, 1955.

Maltby, Major-General C. M. 'Operation in Hong Kong from 8 to 25 December, 1941', *Supplement to London Gazette,* 1941.

Marsman, J. H. *I Escaped from Hong Kong,* New York, 1942.

Maxwell, D. *Ports of the World,* London, 1961.

Meyer, F. V. *Britain's Colonies in World Trade,* Oxford, 1948.

Mills, L. A. *British Rule in Eastern Asia,* Oxford, 1942.

Morgan, F. W. *Ports and Harbours,* London, 1958.

Morse, H. B. *The Chronicles of the East India Company Trading to China 1635–1843,* London, 1929.

Oram, R. B. and Baker, C. C. R. *The Efficient Port,* Oxford, 1971.

Owen, Sir David. *Future Control and Development of the Port of Hong Kong,* 1941.

Pennell, W. V. *History of the Hong Kong General Chamber of Commerce, 1861–1961,* Hong Kong, 1961.

Remer, C. F. *A Study of Chinese Boycotts,* London, 1933.

Roxby, B. M. (ed.). *China Proper,* Geographical Handbook Series, London, 1944.

Salisbury, P. R. 'Comparative Container Ship Design', *Shipping World and Shipbuilder,* Vol. 161, No. 3821, 1968, p. 951–4.

Sargent, A. J. *Anglo-Chinese Commerce and Diplomacy,* Oxford, 1907.

Sargent, A. J. *Seaports and Hinterland,* London, 1938.

Smailes, A. E. *The Geography of Towns,* London, 1957.

Szczepanik, E. *The Economic Growth of Hong Kong,* London, 1958.

Tai Koo Dockyard and Engineering Company of Hong Kong Ltd., *Fifty Years of Shipbuilding and Repairing in the Far East,* Hong Kong, 1954.

Tregear, T. R. and Berry, L. *The Development of Hong Kong and Kowloon as Told in Maps,* Hong Kong, 1959.

Ward, R. S. *Asia for the Asiatics,* Chicago, 1945.

INDEX